Poppies To Paston

The author

Poppies To Paston

A Norfolk Boyhood

by
Robert Bagshaw

I am grateful to the many people who have helped in the production
of this volume of memoirs. Most of all, however, I acknowledge
the support and encouragement of my wife, to whom this book is
dedicated

"I have had playmates, I have had companions,
In my days of childhood, in my joyful school-days –
All, all are gone, the old familiar faces."

FD 382504

Charles Lamb.

L. BAG

© Robert Bagshaw 1986
First published 1986

ISBN   Hardback: 0 900616 21 0
          Paperback: 0 900616 22 9

Printed and published by
Geo. R. Reeve Ltd., Damgate, Wymondham, Norfolk

Contents

Illustrations

Introduction

It was William Shakespeare, of course, who so vividly defined the seven Ages through which Man progresses during his lifetime, all the way from puking babyhood to toothless senility. His acute observation of the steadily changing periods in our development is such as to make them readily recognisable to those of us who have passed through them, and I would certainly have no wish to enter into dispute with the immortal bard. In spite of this, however, I have a firm conviction that the brief sojourn on Earth of the average person can be even more simply divided into just three stages.

The first is represented by childhood and early youth, when we are inclined to live simply for the Present and to take each day as it comes. At that time, the Future is a long way away and, furthermore, we have enjoyed too little of life to realise that there is such a thing as a Past. Then, as the years go by, we become increasingly aware of the importance of the Future and, if we are wise, we take certain steps to ensure that the coming years will bring us the kind of life which we would wish. It is much later in life that we enter upon our third stage and it is then that, with frightening inevitability, we become aware that the greater part of our life is represented by the Past. I have to admit that, though the Present continues to give me great delight and I still have a multitude of ambitions for the Future, my state of maturity is such that I now find myself in that third stage.

It was in this frame of mind that I sat down to record a few reminiscences of my early life. I must make it clear that, when I first put pen to paper, it was purely for personal pleasure and I had no intention of inflicting my memoirs on a wider public. It was only later that, as my memory drew back its curtain on the past and brought a wealth of earlier images flooding into my brain, I gradually became aware that those images were not merely providing me with a nostalgic ego-trip. They brought with them the sudden realisation that our lifestyle in the Norfolk countryside of the twenties and thirties was not only far removed from that which exists today. It was, in fact, a completely different world.

Certain features of our life in those early years find a parallel in today's society, notably such things as high unemployment and the degree of poverty which still exists in some quarters. At that time, however, there was no Welfare State to help the deprived, but merely the disgrace of Poor Law charities for those most in need. In compensation, however, we lived in a loving, caring society where the strong bond of family life was reflected throughout the community. It is true that a working man's wage stayed the same from year to year, but so also did the prices of goods in the shops. The word "inflation" did not exist in our vocabulary, except perhaps in reference to what we did to our bicycle tyres. Aniseed balls, which cost twopence per

7

quarter when I made my first purchase, remained at the same price long after the development of a more discerning palate drew me away from such childish delights.

To chronicle the changes which have taken place during the last fifty years would require the pages of an entire volume. Suffice to say that anybody who has lived through that period must surely have witnessed a greater transformation than at any other similar period in history. The great advances which have been made in both science and technology have inevitably led us into a more materialistic society, far removed from the simple, undemanding life-style of yesteryear. Above all, we lived our lives at a leisurely pace which contrasts strongly with the frenetic, time-watching routine of today.

Our fastest mode of travel was the railway train, for the few motor cars which plied the streets travelled at a somewhat modest pace. I recall the occasion when a group of us, as young lads, discussed the report that a motor race at Brooklands had been won by a car travelling at sixty miles per hour. Being mathematical wizards, we soon deduced that this, in fact, was one mile per minute, and we digested the fact with a strong feeling of incredulity. Nowadays, of course, to travel on a motorway at that speed would most probably incur the wrath of other road users, together with accusations of dawdling.

The three main centres which were the background of my boyhood have been affected to greatly differing degrees by the changes which have overtaken society in the past half-century. Norwich, of course, has seen the greatest transformation with the city's agricultural roots finally yielding to the demands of technology and commerce. There is still much that is beautiful in the old city, though one cannot help wondering whether George Borrow would be quite so fulsome in his praise if he were able to pay it a return visit.

Cromer has changed little. The sea which, in an earlier century, had taken the original settlement of Shipden into its keeping, still dominates the lives of the townsfolk. Cromer's heart still beats in the old, flint-built cottages of the fishing village and sends its pulse radiating out into the seaside resort which surrounds it.

When it comes to a question of heart, however, there is nowhere quite like North Walsham, for there one finds a degree of warmth which I have always found to be unique. The town itself has, happily, never outgrown its atmosphere of quaint rural charm and the ravages of time have failed to destroy the sincerity of its people. Even today, though many of the residents are strangers to me, North Walsham still welcomes me with the same feeling of warm sincerity which was so evident in the days of my boyhood.

Thus, though our world has become a very different place in the last half-century, there is much that still remains unchanged. It is my sincere hope that the pages which follow, whilst giving younger readers an insight into our style of life in those earlier years, will also evoke memories of the past for those of more mature years who were fortunate enough to live through them.

CHAPTER 1

In The Beginning

My father was one of the greatest men I ever knew. By that, I do not mean that he achieved widespread fame or amassed vast amounts of material wealth, for he did neither of those. His passage through life was never likely to make headline material, being at all times clothed in a cloak of modesty and understanding which came from his inner self. Then, when it finally reached its end, he had achieved the greatest prize of all – the love and respect of his fellow men.

He was a journalist by profession and, as such, the world was his oyster and the people he met were the pearls within. He walked with them all on level terms for, although he would never have put such a belief into words, he looked upon all men as equals. The knight in his castle received no greater favour than the fisherman in his cottage, for he enjoyed the company of all. A morning spent in the magistrates' court, an afternoon at a council meeting and an evening on his beloved bowling green – wherever he went he was a friend among friends. I am convinced that he went through his entire life without making a single enemy on the way.

It was an age of tightly-knit families, and ours was no exception. Every action and experience of any one member was a matter of concern to all the others. Each incident in our daily lives, no matter how trivial, became a stitch in the closely-woven family tapestry. It was, in fact, a wonderful example of what a later commanding officer of mine would have called a "tight little ship". Furthermore, if it is true that my father was the captain of the ship, then it can equally be said that my mother was the navigator. Indeed, there were numerous occasions when, but for the steadying influence of my mother's hand on the tiller, our little ship could well have been in danger of foundering.

My father made his steady way through life savouring every minute as it came along. My mother, however, was the planner. For her the important thing was "the future". The present gave her pleasure, but it was her forward planning and the ambitions which she had for us all which dominated her thinking. By the time she had brought four sons into the world she had become outnumbered by five to one in an almost all-male household. Far from being deterred, however, she proudly took up the challenge and concentrated her life on what she always called "my boys". When one of us achieved some little success, my father basked in a radiant glow of pleasure and reflected that life was good. My mother, however, was already looking ahead to the next challenge.

At this point in my narrative I must pause and go even further back in time, for my story really begins some years before my mother appeared on the scene. My father, in fact, was a young lad of fourteen, just leaving school and taking his first tentative steps into an adult world.

The year was 1903 and Edward VII was on the throne of England. Lord Kitchener had just brought the Boer War to a successful conclusion with the resultant incorporation of the Transvaal and the Orange Free State into the British Empire. Mr. Balfour had taken Lord Salisbury's place at the head of the government, and it was to be only a few years before the electorate were to change their allegiance and bring the Liberals to power with a sweeping victory.

Such stirring events, however, must have figured only lightly in the mind of young Arthur Bagshaw as he went through the doors of the London and Norwich Press to take up his post as office boy. His strongest emotion at that time must surely have been one of thankfulness at having found employment. Little did he know that, as he went into that building, he was entering a world which was to dominate his entire life – the world of "The Press".

His father was a dealer in fish, game and poultry, the latest of a long succession of Bagshaws who, over many generations, had represented that trade in the commercial life of the city of Norwich. The young Arthur, however, had his sights set in a different direction and, anyway, there were brothers to carry on the family tradition. He knew what he wanted and he soon showed his seniors that he was not content to be a mere office boy. His talent for writing, coupled with his eagerness to get hold of a good story, soon became apparent, and it was not long before he became a sort of cub reporter. In later years he took great delight in recalling the events of this period of his life, but I think one story will be sufficient to indicate his enthusiasm for his chosen calling.

It concerned the affairs of Norwich City Football Club, which at that time was not the professional organisation which it is today.

Adherence to a strictly amateur code was rigidly enforced and no person connected with the club, least of all a player, was permitted to receive financial benefit from such a connection. At the time in question, however, the first signs of an impending scandal swept through the city with the allegation that the club had been paying some of its players for their services on the pitch. If such an allegation could be substantiated, there can be no doubt that it would have meant the end of Norwich City Football Club.

It was a time for quick action and, accordingly, an emergency meeting was called, the scene of which was to be the upper room in a local hostelry. The meeting was to be held in complete secrecy and members of the Press were barred from attending. My father was not prepared to accept this and, on the fateful night, he was there in the midst of the crushing throng of men pushing their way up that back staircase. Somehow he managed to gain entry to the room unnoticed and there he squeezed himself into a corner and waited excitedly for the revelations which would provide him with his story. Then, at the appointed time, the chairman called the meeting to order, but it was at that moment that my father's world fell tumbling around him. Somebody had recognised him, and the cry went through the room, "There's a reporter among us".

In later years he would chuckle with glee and his eyes would sparkle as he recalled how he was physically ejected from the room and thrown bodily down the stairs. "No", he would say. "I didn't get what I was after, but I went back to the office with a damn good story."

It was inevitable that, with a combination of enthusiasm and natural flair, he should soon outgrow the tag of mere "reporter" and become accepted as a fully fledged journalist. This fact, furthermore, did not pass unnoticed and before long he was given the chance of a transfer to North Norfolk, where he was to apply his talents to the production of the local publication of the day, the "Cromer Post".

This appointment, though accepted with enthusiasm by my father, was not without its problems, for he was a single man and it would be necessary for him to live in the area. However, he had already chosen his life partner in the shape of Emily Mace, the daughter of a well-known boot and shoe retailer. Thus it was that my father and mother married on October 18th 1910.

They began their married life in Suffield Park House and it was there in 1912 that they brought their first child into the world. It

My parents at the time of their marriage in 1910

was a boy and, following the custom of the day, he was given his father's name. The arrival of the young Arthur was heralded with much rejoicing in the family and nobody was more excited than Grandfather Bagshaw, who immediately made the long journey from Norwich in his horse-drawn brougham to inspect his first grandson.

In later years, the fact that Arthur was my parents' first-born child was destined to have a marked effect on my own life, for we always had much in common. We shared the same interests and emotions and, in spite of the age difference, there has always been a strong bond between us. It was he who sowed the first seeds which aroused my interest in nature and the countryside, an interest which we still share. As we reached adult life, we were both destined to enter the same profession and now, in our maturity, I still regard him not merely as my brother but as my closest friend.

Thirteen months after Arthur's arrival on the family scene, my mother gave birth to a second son, Stanley, who was to become the genius of the family. Early signs of the latent talent of the young prodigy were amply confirmed in later years when, joining his father's profession, he graced every facet of his craft and became arguably one of the greatest journalists ever to sit in an editor's chair. His command of languages was legendary, as was his constant striving for understanding amongst the ordinary people of the world.

There was sadness in our family when he was taken from us with barely half his adult life behind him, but our grief was eased by the knowledge that it was shared by the wide circle of people who had been fortunate enough to know him.

At the time of my narrative, however, the future was unknown, and my parents were happy in the house at Suffield Park with their two infant sons. My father, though busily engaged in newspaper matters, found time to cultivate his vegetable garden and also to engage in his greatest passion, his racing pigeons. These he would take to the railway station for dispatch to distant parts on race days. Then there would be the seemingly interminable wait for the first glimpse of the leader returning in tiring flight to its loft. If duty had called him from home, my mother would have been given strict instructions to carry out this task. It was so important to him that, at the time, it took precedence over all else, and my mother shared his happiness.

Soon, however, a dramatic change was to take place as storm clouds gathered over Europe and the world was about to be plunged into the bloodiest of all wars. In the cities, women went to work in the factories, but in the country they went on to the land to replace the men who had been forced to exchange the Norfolk fields for those of Flanders. My father was rejected for military service because of poor eyesight, and he became a special constable. I have always been thankful that my father's eyes did not reach the required standard for soldiering. Without that defect, he might well have suffered the same cruel fate which befell so many of his friends and, quite apart from anything else, I would not now be telling my story.

As the war pursued its relentless course, other factors were occupying the minds of my parents, as a result of which they were to leave their first home. Firstly, my father was required to take charge of the Press Office in Cromer, which would mean living in the town. Then there was the question of education for the two little boys. They were steadily approaching the age of entry into school and the nearest one was a long way away. Thus it was that the four of them took their leave of Suffield Park and set up home in Cromer at the rambling house in Church Street which was later to be the scene of my earliest memories.

This was in 1917, and the war still had more than a year to run. During that time, while my father combined Press work with his constabulary duties, my mother suddenly found herself with many more mouths to feed when the War Office decided that a group of soldiers should be billeted in the house. There must have been times when she found conditions difficult to cope with, but letters which she received after their departure to the Western Front bear testimony to the fact that she mothered them as wholeheartedly as if they had been her own sons.

Then, in June 1918, with the Armistice still only a dream of the future, she presented my father with a third son. This was Peter, and it has always been my firm belief that he was the one of us who mostly inherited the moral characteristics and attitude to life of our father. Not only did he enter the world of journalism, but he also held the same views concerning the people with whom he shared his days. Any ambitiousness in his nature was always under a firm degree of control. If promotion was to mean leaving the district and the people with whom he was happy, then such promotion inevitably came off second best. Above everything, he was a reporter who was trusted by all, for he would never disclose a confidence or endanger a friendship for the sake of a sensationalistic story.

November 1918 was to see the end of the war, and the whole world yearned for a return to normality. In the Church Street household life went on in a kind of ordered chaos for, although the two youngest children were now well settled in at school, my mother's hands were full. Washing and cleaning, sewing and knitting occupied her every moment, especially when my father's absence made it necessary for her to ensure the smooth running of the office.

At that point in her life it seems only natural that there should have been odd moments when she reflected upon how nice it would have been if one of her children had been a girl. She doted upon her sons and always vowed that she would never have parted with any one of them, but it would have been nice to have a little girl.

Consequently, when, in the early weeks of 1920, she knew that there was a fourth child on the way, her hopes began to rise that this would be a daughter. Surely, after three boys, this one really must be a girl.

The facts which I am now reporting do not, of course, arise from first-hand knowledge, but come purely from hearsay. Nevertheless, I am reliably informed that half the population of Cromer joined in my mother's wish and eagerly awaited the day of the birth.

Eventually, that day arrived and Dr. Grant was sent for. Even he, being family friend as much as doctor, knew of my mother's hopes. He took charge of the situation and, in due course, standing by the bed in that upper room, he turned to my mother.

"I'm sorry", he said, "It's another boy. Shall I send it back?"

Back came the reply, "Oh, no. I think I might as well keep him".

I am rather glad she did, for I feel sure there is no need to say that the little boy lying in the good doctor's hands was me.

CHAPTER 2

Poppies and Lifeboats

There is no way of knowing the duration of my parents' disappointment at not having a daughter. I am told that my father had to suffer the jibes of his colleagues concerning the progress he was making towards his own football team, and certainly it is true that ten days had passed before he registered my birth. I prefer to think, however, that this was either through pressure of business or, perhaps, because they had not settled on a name for me. I know not whether they had gone so far as to select a girl's name in advance, for this has always been a closely guarded secret. A name for another boy, however, presented certain problems.

With the arrival of their eldest son, they had followed the Victorian tradition of using tried and trusted family names. With the second and third they had shown a touch of modernity in choosing completely new ones. If they had then reverted to the old tradition I might well have been called Albert, or Ernest, or even Abraham. Eventually the problem was solved for them; or perhaps I should say partially solved.

There was an old family friend by the name of Bob Kimm and, on my arrival, he expressed the wish that I should be named after him. My parents were very fond of him and certainly had no wish to hurt him in any way, but somehow the name Bob did not appeal to them. Accordingly, a compromise was reached and I was christened Geoffrey Robert. Where the name Geoffrey came from remains a mystery, but it mattered little, for few people have ever called me that. Bob Kimm was a frequent visitor and would enter the house with "How's my little Bobby?" Then, as he bounced me on his knee, he would make a point of repeating my name at frequent intervals until everybody forgot the Geoffrey part and accepted me simply as Bobby.

There was to be only one period in my life when this was to cause any real problems. This was when, at the age of eleven, I entered Lakenham School, in Norwich, and was listed on the register simply as Geoffrey Bagshaw. The trouble was that, when the teachers addressed remarks to "Geoffrey", I failed to realise that they were talking to me and I had great difficulty in explaining that it was not inattentiveness which made me fail to respond. Apart from this, however, and a few occasional queries on such things as official forms, I have been quite content to go through life with my second name taking precedence over my first.

At the time of my arrival on the scene, Cromer was endeavouring to re-establish itself as a health resort after the deprivations of the Great War. Its earlier success in this respect had been brought about by the coming of the railway, almost at the turn of the century. This in turn had led to the building of the large hotels and the streets of boarding houses which had completely transformed the aspect of the town. For the four years of war, however, these buildings saw few visitors for there were not many people with the inclination to spend a holiday on the east coast. With the coming of peace there was a gradual return to the vigour and prosperity of the pre-war era. The railways brought the holidaymakers, and the hotels and guest houses opened their doors to receive them. Even my mother showed her willingness to take in paying guests. After all, she had looked after soldiers during the war. Now she was prepared to provide the same service for the pleasure-seekers who were gradually finding their way back to Cromer.

I was naturally unaware of the changes which were taking place outside, but they were to have their effect on my early life and, furthermore, they were to add colour to my present memories of my first years. Memory is one of the most precious of all one's possessions, but it can also be somewhat unreliable. I doubt whether anybody has yet decided at what age the human mind is capable of retaining genuine memory. Certainly, one is inclined to recall early events about which one has merely been told and, after the information has been stored for a time in one's mind, there is a tendency for it later to be recounted as a "memory". For that reason, I can only say that my earliest recollections of my life in Cromer stem not so much from actual events as from sights and smells and sounds.

Thus, I recall the sight and the smell of steam filling the back kitchen as my mother prepared for "a big wash". The huge copper had to be heated in advance and, as the steam rose and the water gurgled, my mother instinctively knew when conditions were right for the materials which had to be boiled. Boiling was necessary in those days, for there were no advanced biological powders or magical fabric conditioners. Boiling, furthermore, did no harm, for most of the items inside the steaming copper were made of good solid

My Mother's Quartet

While Arthur (seated) and Stanley had graduated to Sunday-best suits
and Peter sports the obligatory sailor outfit, I still retain the woollen
dress and little-girl hairdo of a two-year-old

My First Haircut

On Cromer beach with my mother and brothers Stanley (standing) and Peter.
Note the bathing machines in the background

materials like calico and cambric and cotton. Inside that misty kitchen, however, my mother was not entirely without mechanical aids for there, in the corner, stood a piece of apparatus which proclaimed itself to be the "Acme Super Prestige Wringer and Roller". This was, of course, the mangle which removed excess water before the washing was finally dried on the backyard line or, in bad weather, in front of the cooking range.

The front part of the ground floor of the house was given over to business, for this was the Press Office, the very nerve-centre of my father's activities. Here, our senses of sight, smell and touch were continually activated by the material which was the very life-blood of our existence – paper. Paper in all its forms was there but, in particular, newsprint, for there were always piles of newspapers stacked against the walls. Then there was the paper on which my father meticulously wrote out his "copy", together with the special envelopes into which it was put for its journey by rail to the editorial office in Norwich. When I became older, I was often entrusted with the task of taking these precious envelopes to the station and ensuring that they caught the specified train.

Though the "Eastern Daily Press" had the main claim on my father's journalistic activities, he also did his "lineage" for various national newspapers and journals. He received his salary from the Norfolk News Company, whilst the other publications rewarded him with a certain sum (usually one penny) for each line of his writings which they published. Thus, a wide range of daily and weekly papers came into the office and many of these, after perusal by my father, found their way into our hands. Most of them had their regular children's sections which vied with each other for the favouritism of the younger generation. I was particularly fond of Uncle Oojah, whose activities, if my memory serves me correctly, were detailed in the News Chronicle. Uncle Oojah was, in fact, an elephant, but this did not prevent him from regularly sending me a card on my birthday.

We were all fond of Pip, Squeak and Wilfred, who appeared in the Daily Mirror. We followed their adventures with great enthusiasm, and there was particular excitement when it was announced that, as part of a nationwide tour, they would be visiting Cromer. On the great day, a large crowd of children had assembled to greet the intrepid trio on their arrival in Town and then, in Pied Piper fashion, we followed as they made their way to the sea front. For the benefit of the uninitiated perhaps I should explain that Pip was a dog, Squeak a penguin and Wilfred a rabbit. Thus it was that, on seeing that vast expanse of sea, Squeak decided that it was an opportunity not to be missed, and he took off across the beach. For a while panic gripped both the watchers and the organisers until the penguin was eventually surrounded and brought back into the company of his friends. My memory of this incident is, to say the least, hazy, for I was extremely young at the time. I rely, in fact, solely upon information supplied by my eldest brother, Arthur, for I was in his charge at the time, being propelled by him in my pushchair as we followed the cavalcade.

In view of my tender years, it is not surprising that most of my early recollections should reflect our home life and, furthermore, should involve my mother. Thus it is that I see her, having completed her big wash, working away on her ironing table in the little room at the top of the stairs. Then, in the evening, I would hear her knitting needles chattering away in ceaseless rhythm as she sat by the fire in the parlour. If I now shut my eyes, I can picture her gently rubbing Snowfire on my chilblains and plying me with senna pod tea to safeguard my "inner cleanliness". I doubt whether life really was as simple as that, but that is the way my memory insists on bringing it back to me.

Overshadowing all personal trivia, however, there were two ever-present features which could not fail to dominate the memory of anybody who has lived in the area, namely poppies and lifeboats.

To my infant mind it seemed that the poppies were alway there. This, of course, was not so, but every year they reappeared in such rampant profusion as to paint the landscape with vast splashes of crimson. It was no accident that the area around Cromer became known as "Poppyland". It was, furthermore, no accident that Clement Scott should choose it as the setting for his verses "The Garden of Sleep" which were to bring the beauty of the district to a much wider public. It was only a mile or two down the road, at Sidestrand, that Scott and his celebrated colleagues had found relaxation in the Miller's House. Indeed, in my childhood, the Garden of Sleep was still there, nestling at the edge of the cliff in the shadow of the ruined church tower. There are not so many poppies now, of course, but, whenever Man gives them a fair chance, they still flaunt their beauty as if in celebration of past glory.

If the appearance of the poppies was seasonal by nature, the same could not be said of the lifeboats, for they were likely to be called into action at any time. There have been lifeboats at Cromer since 1804 and, as the world knows, there has never been a shortage of volunteers to man them.

For the greatest part of its existence, Cromer had been just a little fishing village and, in essence, this has never changed. It is true that it has grown the brick shell of the railway-age seaside resort, but its true heart still remains within the little flint-built cottages where it all began. From these cottages, over so many generations, have come the brave men who, while making their living from the sea, have been ever ready to risk all in bringing help to fellow mariners.

Today's lifeboatmen are as courageous as any who have gone before but, thankfully, they now have boats worthy of their dedication, together with all the advantages of modern technology. In the days of my childhood, however, things were so very different. The *Louisa Heartwell*, a veteran of 21 years' service, was said to be the favourite boat of the crew, who would go anywhere in her. Undoubtedly she was a beautiful craft, but she was basic in the extreme. Above all, in the manner of her predecessors, she relied on men wielding oars to take her about her business, for it was not until 1923 that the first motor-driven lifeboat came to Cromer.

I well remember the *H.F. Bailey* arriving on station, for I was wrapped in warm clothing and taken to the clifftop to witness its first launch. It was a day of great celebration, for it meant that the crew would no longer have to strain at their oars and battle with gales and shallow water to get their craft away from the beach and into the open sea. Their welcome for the new boat was tinged with some regret, however, for the *Louisa Heartwell* had a proud record of service and had earned the deep affection of all who had sailed in her. It is interesting to note that when, in 1923, she was sold, she fetched the princely sum of £55, whilst her successor cost all of £10,500. Nowadays, of course, the provision of a new boat involves an expenditure of hundreds of thousands of pounds.

It would not be completely true to say that the arrival of the *H.F. Bailey* marked the end of the rowing boat at Cromer for, while she became the No. 1 boat, the No. 2 position went to the *Alexandra*. The *Alexandra*, one of the old generation of oar-powered boats, remained in service for a further ten years and, indeed, played a part in one of the most celebrated of Cromer rescue missions when the barge "Sepoy" was wrecked in 1933. This was by no means one of the biggest rescues, for the barge carried a crew of just two men,

The Sepoy Rescue

The two crew members cling to the rigging as the oarsmen of the *Alexandra*
strive to reach the wreck.

Coxswain Henry Blogg brings the *H.F. Bailey* in for the final rescue.

but the entire proceedings took place within 150 yards of the shore and in the sight of several hundred people.

When, just after dawn on that December morning, the barge hoisted its distress signal, the *H.F. Bailey* was already away at Happisburgh on another mission, so it was necessary to launch the *Alexandra*. This proved almost impossible for, in spite of the efforts of a large number of helpers, the wind and waves continually threw the boat back onto the beach. This went on throughout the morning and eventually, in the early afternoon, the oarsmen succeeded in getting the boat out to the stricken barge. Even then, however, rescue was impossible, for a mighty wave threw the lifeboat back towards the shore and, in fact, over the breakwater.

At that fateful moment, the *H.F. Bailey* was spotted returning at full speed from Happisburgh. Even for the motor boat, however, a rescue seemed impossible, for conditions had worsened and it was doubted whether she could get near enough. By skilful manoeuvring, however, the coxswain brought the lifeboat crashing over the hull of the barge and took off, first one, and then the other marooned man. They were brought ashore to scenes of great enthusiasm while the church bells rang out a merry peal.

The coxswain of that lifeboat was, of course, the most illustrious of all lifeboatmen, Henry Blogg. Coxswain Blogg had joined the lifeboat as a young man of twenty and he became the very symbol of the Service until his retirement in 1947. He achieved great fame and received more decorations and awards than any other lifeboatman, but surely his greatest reward was that, during his 53 years of service, the Cromer lifeboats had saved 873 lives. Above all, he earned the love and respect of the people of the Town, and many a man still proudly boasts that he knew Henry Blogg. I regret that I cannot really claim that distinction although I did occasionally spend time in his company. The reason is that my father and he were good friends, and I frequently watched the two men engaged in earnest discussion as they shared each other's company. Unfortunately, I was too young to understand their conversation, although I have since been told that the topic they discussed would most likely have been football.

I could not possibly leave my early memories of Cromer without a mention of its most famous product, the crab. Furthermore, the association between crabs and lifeboats is very strong, for it was the men who ventured out to rescue shipwrecked mariners who, in more routine moments, brought in this harvest of the sea. Cromer crabs are, of course, renowned amongst lovers of shellfish although, in fairness, it must be conceded that those caught at Sheringham are just as good. It was not just the catching of the crabs which was important, however, but also the manner in which they were "dressed" prior to being eaten. This was an art which was acquired at an early age and it was one at which my father was very adept. Thus, he was able to remove the "poison bag" and also to flush out every little portion of meat from the claws, thus ensuring that it was presented in an attractive manner and with a minimum of waste.

I have never mastered the art of crab dressing but, fortunately, my wife has long possessed that skill. Thus I am able to savour the delights of that delicious meat and, at the same time, to let my mind wander back in time to memories of those tender years of my early childhood.

CHAPTER 3
North Walsham

Life in those early days at Cromer proceeded at a very modest pace. The people of the town went about their business in the peaceful, unhurried manner which was typical of the age in which they lived and, apart from the occasional launching of the lifeboat, there was little to disrupt the quiet rhythm of our little world. My father spent his days gathering in the news and, in company with his friend Bob Kimm, cultivating his allotment. My mother, with an appearance of outward calm, busied herself with the task of tending to the needs of her five male dependants. My two eldest brothers were daily attending school, where Peter later joined them. My tender years, however, dictated that I must, for a while, remain within the protection of the family home.

It was behind this facade of apparent peace and routine normality that my mother began to develop the first, and probably the greatest, of all her life's ambitions. It started as a secret longing but gradually, as the years passed, it was to acquire such magnitude in her mind as to supersede almost everything else. It was, in fact, that all four of us should, in due course, attend Sir William Paston's School in North Walsham.

Paston was a school with a long and ancient heritage and was held in high regard as a centre of scholastic excellence. Its pupils were drawn from a wide area of Norfolk, however, and, although scholarships were offered every year, it was not easy to gain acceptance. Nevertheless, in 1923, the first part of my mother's ambition was achieved when Arthur succeeded in convincing the governors that he was a fit and proper person to be admitted within those hallowed walls. The following year Stanley followed in his footsteps, a fact which surprised nobody, for he was a child of inborn brilliance who was destined to become a man of greatness. Thus, within the space of two short years, my mother saw the first half of her great plan reach fruition. The second half was destined to take much longer, however, for Peter was just six years old and I had not even started my schooling.

This, then, was the situation when, in 1925, a major change came

26

over our lives with my father's transfer to the office at North Walsham. Up came our roots and down the road we travelled to the little market town which was to be our home for the next six years. I doubt whether there was any immediate change in our lifestyle, but it was there, during my formative years in the late twenties, that I was to undergo experiences and make friendships which were to colour my memory for the rest of my life.

North Walsham was a pleasant little town which exuded an atmosphere of almost undisturbed peace together with many outward signs of earlier prosperity. Much of the splendour of the town was a legacy from the 14th century weavers who lavished their wealth on such buildings as the parish church. Later prosperity had come with the building of the North Walsham and Dilham Canal, which opened the town to the wider commercial waterways of Britain. Then, of course, the spread of a network of railways over the face of the land improved access even more and we were, in fact, fortunate that two companies ran their rail systems through North Walsham. Thus, we had a pair of stations nestling almost side by side at the edge of the main approach to the town.

By far the more important of these two railways was the London and North Eastern (L.N.E.R.) for, besides connecting with Cromer in the north, it proceeded in the other direction to Norwich and the great network beyond. The lesser of the two, the Midland and Great Northern (M. & G.N. or, as we all knew it, the "Muddle and Get Nowhere") connected us with the coast at Great Yarmouth, and, in the other direction, swung across through Aylsham to Melton Constable, which was the great railway centre of Norfolk. We did very little rail travelling in those early days and, on the L.N.E.R., we made just the occasional trip to Norwich to visit relatives. My father's racing pigeons, however, were more frequent travellers, for they regularly made the journey to such places as Birmingham and Manchester which, to us, were just place-names on a map. The M. & G.N. also fulfilled a need, for it called at Hemsby, where we were destined to spend many an annual seaside holiday.

The real heart of North Walsham, however, lay in the Market Place, for it was here that most of the shops and business properties were congregated. Dominating the Market Place at its lower end stood the quaint old Market Cross which had been put there by a Bishop of Norwich in 1550. Its dome-like roof spread out far and wide and gave protection to the ancient fire engine which was

The quaint old Market Cross, built by a Bishop of Norwich in 1550

preserved beneath. This strange little contraption dated back to the eighteenth century and we constantly wondered how it could possibly have been of any use in putting out any major sort of fire. We counted ourselves fortunate that our fire brigade had the most up-to-date of all engines, built on a Model T chassis with solid rubber tyres and the ability to carry a full crew to an outbreak in the shortest possible time.

Most of the shops were small and owner-occupied, though we did have a branch of the Star Supply Stores and also Brenner's Penny Bazaar. This later became Peacock's Bazaar, with everything priced at either threepence or sixpence, and it was eventually superseded, of course, by Woolworth's. Most of the businesses, however, were owned by local people and the personal touch was very much in evidence. Thus, Mr. Loads was the draper, Mr. Randell the ironmonger and Mr. Ling the chemist whilst, in the shadow of the Church, Mr. Jeary had his sweet shop. North Walsham was well served by its tradespeople, who could offer everything which any member of the community might need.

Shopping in those days was a very peaceful occupation when compared with the hurly burly of today. I suppose the two strongest memories one retains of that era are the degree of personal service and the unhurried manner in which each transaction was carried out. Most shopkeepers were always ready to pass the time of day with prospective customers and many, in fact, had chairs

The Market Place, with Mr. Jeary's sweet shop under the awning on the left

Market Street in early traffic-free days

The ancient fire appliance which rested beneath the domed roof
of the Market Cross

We counted ourselves fortunate to have the protection of the
most up-to-date fire engine of the day

strategically placed in front of the counters so that shoppers could rest their weary limbs while their purchases were being prepared. Very few products were pre-packed in those days. One's selected portion of cheese would be tenderly cut from a huge block by means of a length of wire, whilst such things as sugar and tea were weighed out and packed at the time of purchase.

Even the process of paying for one's purchase was carried out in accordance with a long-established routine, particularly in the larger shops. It was not just a question of handing over one's cash and having it thrown into the inner recesses of a till. A hand-written bill was meticulously made out and handed to the customer, who would then proffer her money in payment. The bill and cash were then inserted into a metal cylinder which was attached by the shop assistant to an overhead wire. The pull of a lever would then send it travelling along the wire to the finance department which was situated in an upper room at the back of the shop. Then, after a short pause, the cylinder would come gliding back to the counter, where it would be opened to reveal the receipted bill and the customer's change. As a small boy I was always eager to visit any shop which used this method for, particularly on a busy day, the cylinders seemed to be in perpetual motion as they flew in all directions, rather like a miniature cable-car railway.

The average retailer's attitude to his customers was typified not only by his personal manner, but also by his style of dress. Thus, the ladies in the draper's shop wore neat blouses and long, demure skirts, whilst the grocers covered themselves with long, white aprons, always spotlessly clean. There was always a sense of correctness in matters of dress, and this was reflected in all walks of life.

Even my father conformed to this for, although he was not continually changing his clothing, he had a variety of hats which he wore as occasion demanded. It was not that he derived enjoyment from a change of headgear, but rather that his choice was determined solely by the type of function or event which he was attending. Thus, on informal occasions or, sometimes, when he was engaged in some off-duty pursuit, he would sport a flat cap, whilst such duties as Police Courts would call for the trilby. His most revered headgear, however, was his bowler hat, on which he lavished the greatest care and attention. This was reserved for the more formal occasions, for the mere placing of a bowler on one's head conveyed a very aura of propriety. Thus, his attendance at a funeral or at some function at which gentry or nobility were to be present meant that the bowler was an essential part of his dress.

The bowler hat has now passed largely into oblivion and has become, if anything, a symbol of mirth rather than of respectability. One can, of course, still see it at a meet of the local Hunt or at a point-to-point meeting or agricultural show where, frequently in festive grey, it declares its wearer to be a steward or other high official. In the earlier years of this century, however, it was the very symbol of respectability. To the businessman it gave an air of steadiness, to the foreman responsibility and to the undertaker the necessary degree of sorrowfulness. To my father, above all, it gave a sense of correctness befitting the occasion. In any case, if he was out "on a story", we only needed to glance at the hatstand in the hall to see which item of headgear was missing and we then knew, at least, what type of function he was attending.

I suppose the strongest impression which the casual observer gets when looking at photographs taken in those days of the late twenties is most probably the general drabness of the people's clothing. Certainly it is true that most men and women clung to the tradition of black, grey or, sometimes, brown, for the strictures of austere Victorianism were still firmly rooted in the community. Furthermore, there was little interest in such things as fashion trends and, unlike the ever-changing moods of today's affluent society, the style of dress varied little with the passage of the years. There may well have been a world of fashion in London and other large cities but, for the most part, the country community remained untouched by such trivialities. Furthermore, even those ladies who may have wished to follow any change in fashion would have had great difficulty in so doing, for the general depressed state of the country economy meant that there was little money available for luxuries.

In spite of this, however, great importance was attached to one's manner of dress and, throughout all classes of society, the principles of correctness were rigidly observed. Most manual workers, of course, wore second-best clothes for work, but, even so, they changed into "something better" on returning home and still reserved their very best for Sundays. Workers in the better jobs, such as teachers and clerks, always wore suits and would never have considered entering their place of employment without a clean collar and neatly-knotted necktie. Very few women worked in those days, but those who did, such as shop assistants and teachers, dressed with great propriety. A simple frock was acceptable, although most still adhered to the combination of blouse and skirt which conferred a degree of respectability upon the wearer. No woman, of course, ever wore trousers.

I well remember the sense of shock caused by the introduction some years later of the first "trouser suits" for women. They were apparently intended for holiday wear, for they were known as "beach pyjamas". They were by no means revealing, for they covered every inch of the wearer's body and were made in the most loosely-fitting of styles. The material of which they were made, however, was of the most outlandishly vivid colours, often bearing a design of huge, brightly-coloured flowers. Such things were, of course, never seen in North Walsham, but they caused quite a stir when they were first seen being paraded along the front at Yarmouth. Such innovations would never have found a place in our little community, where conformity was the order of the day.

Even the children had to conform to the accepted standards, and this meant that we were continually ringing the changes through a succession of different articles of apparel. Although there was no uniform, we had a set of clothing which was considered both serviceable and respectable enough for school use, and we also had our "Sunday best". Further down the scale we had our "sitting-about clothes" for indoor use, and then our playing clothes for out-side wear. This last grade of apparel was usually divisible into two for, although almost anything was good enough for playing in one's own garden, our mother would usually insist that we must wear something slightly better if we went out to play elsewhere. It can truly be said that conforming to the accepted standards of dress was a highly complicated business.

Most of the older members of the community rigidly adhered to the dictates of the Victorian era in which they had been brought up, and one such person was my maternal grandmother. She was tall and upright, always stiff and unbending, although I was never quite sure how much of this was due to her physical stature and how much to the restrictive nature of her corsets. These garments, fashioned from a mixture of steel and whalebone, encased her in a vice-like grip which made stooping somewhat difficult and, further-more, caused her to squeak when she walked.

She always dressed in almost unrelieved black, except for a white blouse which peeped out around her neck and which was held in place at the front by a cameo brooch. Her skirts were so long that they almost swept the ground, leaving just sufficient room for her little black boots to be visible underneath. Under her skirts there was room for a wealth of undergarments, for she held strongly to the belief that human flesh was a delicate commodity which must at all times be protected from the cruel air. The most striking articles of her underwear were the thick woollen petticoats which she herself, working interminably in her high-backed chair, crocheted from a vast array of coloured wools. Each of these petticoats called for the use of a large quantity of wool and, when completed, was extremely heavy. One can only marvel at her physical strength in being able to live an active life whilst carrying such a weight of clothing, for she always wore three such petticoats in the winter and never less than two in the summer. Furthermore, the fact that she always appeared to be extremely slim suggests that, when divested of her clothing, she must have presented an extremely light-weight figure.

At this point, lest the reader should wonder how a lad of such tender years should have acquired so intimate a knowledge of his grandmother's underwear, I would hasten to point out that such knowledge was only acquired after the petticoats were finally discarded. Nothing was ever wasted and, consequently, the wool was unravelled from the petticoats, tied in hanks, washed and dried. Then it was cut into pieces of the required length for pegging into canvas in the making of hearthrugs, thus extending its useful life for quite a number of years.

My grandmother was as formal in her dress as she was in her general manner, and she would never venture out of the house without her hat. I only recall her having one hat, which was a large contraption of shiny black straw, decorated with black lace and a brightly-coloured artificial rose. In order to ensure that it stayed on her head, even in the strongest wind, she held it in place by means of three gigantic hat pins which had black knobs on one end and the most vicious-looking sharp points on the other. I frequently watched, fascinated, as she stood before the mirror and, with her face contorted into all possible expressions of pain and discomfort, carefully manoeuvred the pins into place. It was a long process until, with a loud sigh of relief, she would eventually get the final pin into position and declare herself satisfied with the outcome. I continually marvelled at her skill in inserting those murderous-looking objects into one side and out the other without piercing her skull.

Although she would never venture outside without her hat, she was always happy to remove it when she returned. I found this easily understandable when, on one occasion, she handed it to me with the order to take it upstairs and lay it on her bed. As I held it in my hands I was struck by its great weight and I found myself wondering how any human being could possibly carry such a heavy object on her head and still manage to walk upright. She naturally wore the hat for Church on Sundays and on those days it was also her custom to replace her outer petticoat with one of a stiffer black material. She considered this more in keeping with the Sabbath and, what is more, it made a rustling sound as she walked.

It will be seen that my grandmother's mode of dress was typical of the Victorian era in which she had been raised. Within that sombre array of clothing there was the heart of a sweet and gentle lady who, though a strict disciplinarian, was full of kindness and understanding. Outwardly, however, she was a symbol of an age in which nothing ever seemed to change. Even on festive occasions, formality had to be preserved at all costs. Then, following a death and throughout the statutory period of mourning, all she had to do was to remove the rose from her hat and she immediately exhibited the degree of propriety which she considered right and proper. As I now look back over half a century I have to admit that it was, indeed, another world.

It was, furthermore, the world in which I found myself when we left Poppyland and put down our roots in our new home, "Woodland View".

CHAPTER 4

"Woodland View"

"Woodland View" was a somewhat rambling old house which stood by the side of Kimberley Road near its junction with Lime Tree Road. Kimberley Road linked up with Bacton Road at its western end but in the other direction, after it had passed our house, it just petered out into nowhere. The land beyond, now covered by a modern housing estate, was simply a wilderness of scrub and meadow. This, together with the large garden which surrounded our house, was a veritable wonderland of boyhood delight which always had something new to offer us as we explored its treasures.

To be factually correct, "Woodland View" was one of a pair of semi-detached houses which stood sideways to the road. It was, in fact, necessary for us to pass through the garden of the other house, called "Royston View", in order to reach our front door. For the most part, however, we used one of the many gaps in the hedge which gave direct access to our part of the garden. On the occasions when we did pass through our neighbour's garden, we did so with a full measure of propriety, for he was a man who instinctively commanded our respect. He was Mr. Welby, and he was a dentist. Actually, his full name was Mr. Lepine Whalebelly. We never could understand why Whalebelly was pronounced Welby, but that was the way it was.

I would hasten to say that it was not the nature of Mr. Welby's occupation which caused us to view him with a feeling of awe, for we had no reason to fear his professional attentions. On one occasion, at a very early age, I was taken to him for the extraction of an aching tooth, after which he described me to my mother as "a brave little boy". I well remember the feel of his needle being inserted into my gum (an action which, at the time, I thought was carried out in order to loosen the tooth) and then the quick twist as the offending molar was removed. I certainly had no cause to associate him with pain.

Our respect for him was engendered by the manner in which he conducted himself, for he was tall and upright in his bearing and his facial expression, though seldom really stern, never relaxed into anything resembling a smile. Furthermore, we were constantly in fear of the action he might take if we allowed our tennis balls to land in his garden. Whenever such an accident happened, we knew better than to go and retrieve it without first asking him for his permission. He would always allow us to go and collect it, but he would inevitably add the rider, "If it comes over again, I shall confiscate it". We had no idea of the meaning of the word "confiscate", and we imagined all sorts of terrible fates which might befall our ball if it fell into that forbidden territory. Thus, for a while, our games became rather tense affairs as we struggled to ensure that the ball remained within bounds.

When the tension became too great, we would adjourn to another part of the garden and take up some other activity. It was never difficult to find an alternative pastime, for both garden and house had much to offer our growing family. I often think that cleaning and heating the house must have given my mother many problems, but we were never aware of this. Certainly, my father was always active for, in moments away from his work, he had ample scope for cultivating his vegetables and tending his hens whilst, at the back of the house, he had a loft for his beloved pigeons. The constant cooing of those birds was one of the sounds which became deeply woven into my childhood memories, for there were only occasional days when the loft was silent. That was when my father sent them away for a race. Then he would place them lovingly in a travelling cage which he would strap on the back of his bicycle and, riding off to the railway station, he would put them on a train destined for some distant part of the country. Then there would be no sound from the loft until, in the fullness of time, the birds would find their way back to the sanctuary of our garden.

My father's gardening activities ensured that we were more or less self-supporting as regards vegetables, and we also had a large orchard which provided a constant supply of apples and pears. There were loganberries, too, and raspberries, both red and yellow. We had never seen yellow raspberries before. One of the most valuable plots, however, was the one where the artichokes grew for, although they were never harvested, their long sturdy stalks made superb arrows for firing from our home-made bows. These missiles would fly straight and true and cover vast distances down the entire length of our garden. There was, however, one disastrous occasion which was to result in their use being banned by our parents.

It involved Charlie Rump, who had come round to play with Peter and me, and it was Peter who was the unfortunate marksman. He was demonstrating the fire power of our weapons and, as the arrow flew from his bow, it must have hit some undetected thermal. Anyway, it suddenly deviated from its course and, giving no time for evasive action, promptly hit Charlie in the left eye. The effect was catastrophic. Charlie gave vent to a phantom-like shriek and fell to the ground as though mortally wounded. Worse still, his eye immediately took on the vivid hues of a glowing autumn sunset. Panic seized us all, and there was only one thing to be done – call our mother. Actually, there was no need to call her, for, having heard Charlie's cry, she was already trotting towards us. There was little she could do apart from clucking consolingly over the prostrate figure until, very gradually, his howling calmed down to a somewhat muted sobbing. Eventually, Charlie proclaimed that he wanted to go home but, before allowing him to do so, our mother announced that she had something for him to take with him. She then proceeded to cut him a bunch of flowers, which struck us as being a rather odd gift for a small boy who had just been mortally wounded. It was only later that we realised that it was intended as a peace offering to Charlie's mother.

In the days that followed, Charlie's eye progressed through a variety of shades of black and blue and purple until, a few weeks later, normality returned. Charlie enjoyed every minute of it, for he was allowed to attend school wearing a black eye-patch which made him very much the centre of attraction to the other boys. Sadly for us, however, no more arrows were ever fired and, as season followed season, the artichoke stalks remained uncut.

During those days at "Woodland View" we had a number of cats which led an idyllic life patrolling both house and outbuildings and making steady inroads into the rodent population. It would be difficult to say exactly how many cats we had at any given time. Officially there were only two but, because of their free-ranging activities, sudden increases occurred with monotonous regularity. Then, after every population explosion, there would be frantic canvassing in an effort to find homes for the new arrivals. My father could never bring himself to destroy a life and I sometimes think we must have supplied the greater part of North Walsham with feline ratcatchers.

My father's belief in the sanctity of life was never better

exemplified than in his treatment of a cockerel which led a privileged life as ruler of our flock of backyard hens. On one sad morning the bird was found to have a broken leg, apparently caused by its having become entangled in the wire netting surrounding the run. With many people, I suppose, that would have been the end of the creature's existence, but that was not my father's way. He immediately set to work with a system of splints to try and heal the fracture. Unfortunately, his efforts met with no success, but still he was undeterred. Out came his penknife and, using a branch from the hedgerow, he carved a wooden leg which he proceeded to fix to the bird's withered stump. The result was dramatically successful and, for the next two years, that cockerel continued to lord it over his hens like some kind of avian Long John Silver.

The animal which always had pride of place in our affections, however, was our dog, Bonzo. Bonzo was officially declared to be an Airedale Terrier and we always described him as such. Looking back, however, one cannot help thinking that his degree of conformity with that particular breed was, to say the least, slightly tenuous. Certainly, the characteristics of the Airedale were there, but so also were a variety of other features which hinted strongly at a multiplicity of strains amongst his earlier antecedents.

Bonzo was, above all, a great swimmer. There were times, in fact, when he seemed more in his element in the water than on land. When my father took us on boating trips on the Broads, Bonzo would jump overboard and swim behind the boat. His reaction when we first took him to the seaside at Bacton was one of unconcealed delight at that vast expanse of water. He spent the entire day swimming and, even then, needed much coaxing back to land when it was time for the journey home.

His first experience of the seaside was to have a sequel in the days that followed. It was a five-mile journey to Bacton and the reason why we had taken Bonzo was that we had been driven there by a friend who actually owned a motor car – a rare treat! Well, the next day Bonzo went missing and he had still not returned by nightfall. The following morning, however, he was sitting on the front doorstep eagerly awaiting signs of activity within. We would probably never have known the secret of his truancy if my father had not later encountered a friend in the town and been greeted with the remark, "Your Bonzo was having a fine time on the beach at Bacton yesterday". From then onwards, Bonzo frequently made the ten-mile round trip to the seaside, where he soon became a familiar part of the local scene.

Those days of the middle and late twenties were, above all, days of peace and harmony, with just the occasional hiccup to disrupt the smooth flow of everyday life. On reflection, I now find that fact surprising, for conditions among the adult population were extremely difficult. Above all, the average working man's pay was scandalously low, a fact which meant that the housewife's weekly budget had to be carefully controlled to the last halfpenny, or even farthing. Most farm workers received sixpence an hour for a fifty hour week and my father, who was better paid than most, received a mere four pounds weekly. Furthermore, there were no automatic increases and most workers laboured year after year for the same wage.

One cannot help thinking that, in some ways, the expectations and aspirations of most working men had advanced little since the nineteenth century. Above all, however, they were more contented in those days, and the widespread deprivation certainly did not lead to an increase in criminal tendencies. Nobody considered it necessary to lock the door when leaving the house and, if one forgetfully left such a thing as a bicycle in a public thoroughfare, it would still be there the next day.

It was all a question of managing as best one could and of looking on the bright side. I recall my mother telling me of the time when the husband of a friend of hers had been injured at work and, in consequence, had lost his job. Almost immediately, however, the woman had managed to find a position for her young daughter "in service". "Truly", declared the woman, "When the good Lord shuts one door, He opens up another"!

The greatest controlling factor in family life was, in many ways, the housewife's purse, for the activities of the week were largely governed by the amount of money it contained. Every penny had to be wisely spent and any saving which presented itself was eagerly seized upon. It has to be admitted that, in those days, most men were smokers, for it was one of the few pleasures which were readily available. Even there, however, savings could be made for, while a packet of ten cigarettes cost sixpence, the larger pack of twenty could be bought for 11½d. Even that halfpenny represented a significant saving.

Local tradespeople, particularly such as drapers and haberdashers, fully realised the attraction which an apparent bargain had for their customers. Thus, if an article was to be sold for two shillings, they would include a little packet of pins or needles. By this means, the price could be declared as "one and elevenpence three farthings and a farthing change in pins".

I well remember an exciting day when the postman brought to our house a postcard which was addressed to my mother and which bore simply the cryptic message:

"Something for nothing. How can it be true?
The postman tomorrow will bring it to you."

Sure enough, the postman called again on the next day and presented her with the promised package. We all gathered round as she tore open the wrapper to reveal inside a little tin of biscuits. I doubt whether the gift was worth more than sixpence, but I know she felt an inward glow of pleasure as she held it up for all to see.

Such gifts from manufacturers were not very common, but there was one product in particular, the Oxo cube, which was the source of many such offerings. At that time each individual Oxo cube was enclosed inside its own little cardboard wrapper and, if one collected the requisite number of these wrappers, one could exchange them for a gift. My mother was always a great maker of gravy, which we consumed in vast quantities. I honestly believe that, during her lifetime, she must have made enough gravy to float an ocean liner. There was a very good reason for this, for our main meal of the day was taken in two parts – first the pudding and then the meat. Thus she would make huge Yorkshire puddings (or sometimes dumplings) and we would each receive a large helping absolutely swimming in Oxo gravy. The theory was that, before we came to the meat, the edge would have been taken off our appetite and we would not need such a large helping. After all, a joint of meat large enough to last us for two days (one day hot and the next day cold) cost all of four shillings, which represented a fair proportion of her weekly housekeeping money.

Anyway, my mother used Oxo cubes by the hundred and, carefully saving each wrapper, she tied them together with cotton in bundles of fifty. Then we would consult the list of gifts to decide which we would send for. There was quite a wide range, and my mother had a particular liking for the leather bag, for this had such a variety of uses. We had a number of these, one of which hung permanently on the back of the kitchen door and held all the wrappers which were being collected towards the next free gift. To us boys, however, it was the cricket bats and real leather footballs which had the greatest appeal, for they were of the finest quality. In a comparatively short space of time we had consumed sufficient Oxo gravy to enable the four of us each to possess our own bat and ball.

There was another gift which I received in my very early boyhood, and one which came, in fact, from such an unexpected source as to make it doubly memorable. Every Tuesday Mr. Randell, the paraffin man, came trundling along Lime Tree Road with his horse and cart, calling at each house on the way. Eventually he would reach Kimberley Road and my mother would be there to meet him as he brought his vehicle to a halt. I would always be there with her, for I knew that he was not just a paraffin man. Underneath the tarpaulin which covered his cart, in fact, there was always a veritable wealth of treasures spread out under my mother's gaze in the hope that she would be tempted into buying. Nearly always, indeed, there would be things she needed, for he carried Monkey Brand and Lifebuoy soap, gipsy pegs and bootlaces, not to mention bathbrick for the steps and my mother's favourite Lambert's Tea. My mother always favoured Lambert's Tea for she considered it to be the best and, furthermore, if she saved sufficient wrappers she could then exchange them at their shop in Norwich for a free quarter pound of tea.

For me, however, the greatest attraction of Mr. Randell's cart lay under a piece of cloth at the back, for this was where he kept his sweet box. Thus, when my mother had completed her purchases, the cloth would be lifted so that I could view the treasures within. There would be sherbet fountains and long liquorice strings, bags of popcorn and locust seed, and huge ha'penny bullseyes which could be sucked and sucked for hours. Almost unfailingly, if my mother had a spare halfpenny, I would be allowed to make my own selection from this array of delights.

On one particular day, however, I was to receive a totally unexpected surprise when Mr. Randell, in conversation with my mother, suddenly said, "I wonder if young Bobby has been good enough to have a Valentine bag". "I should think so", replied my mother and then, diving his hand into the inner recesses of the cart, Mr. Randell drew out a brown paper bag which he placed in my hands. I was somewhat taken aback but I hope I said "Thank you" for, when I looked inside, my heart pounded at the sight of a collection of little paper packets, all containing unknown objects. I could hardly wait to get indoors to unravel the secret of my unexpected windfall and, as I removed the wrappers, my pleasure knew no bounds. There were two apples in one wrapper, a humbug in another; then a little packet of biscuits and, in the fourth, some sugar-covered sweets.

"Wasn't Mr. Randell kind", I said to my mother, "to give me a Valentine bag."

"No more than he should", she replied, "considering the money I spend with him."

It seems that, every Valentine's Day, he carried such bags for the children of his best customers, and on that particular occasion my turn had at last arrived.

CHAPTER 5

Mixed Infants

North Walsham Council School was typical of so many of the junior educational establishments which were dotted about the county at that time. Larger than most of the village schools, it dominated a corner site overlooking The Park (a mere stretch of grassland), over which it flaunted its aura of Victorian austerity. Always seeming to be unnecessarily tall, its windows were so large that the upper ones could only be opened with the aid of a long, hooked pole or by means of an intricate system of cords and pulleys. These windows certainly served to admit the maximum amount of light, but they did little to conserve any semblance of warmth and comfort, particularly in the winter months.

This lack of consideration for the physical well-being of the inmates was even more evident in the toilet block, a mere assembly of brick walls, open to the elements, which owed nothing to any modern ideas in the way of plumbing or heating. The building was a mere necessity – not the sort of place in which to hang about unnecessarily, especially in the depth of a Norfolk winter.

The entire complex, in fact, was basic in the extreme and designed merely as an assembly point where young minds could be filled with the basics of reading, writing and arithmetic, together with a smattering of such things as history, geography and music. There can be little doubt that such conditions would not be tolerated in today's enlightened society. Nevertheless, my years at the Council School were to be some of the happiest of my life for our teachers, though perhaps not representing the top fruit of the educational tree, did at least spare no effort in filling our lives with love and understanding. Furthermore, as I now look back from a distance, I have the strongest conviction that there could have been no better foundation on which I could build my later life. Not only could I read, write and count, but those dedicated men and women had drawn open a curtain to reveal a wonderland of mystery and enchantment which was life itself.

There were three departments in the school, known individually as "senior boys", "senior girls" and "mixed infants". The entire

44

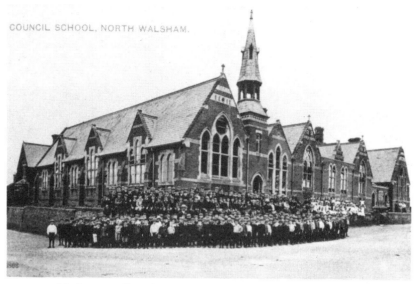

My first seat of learning – the Council School, with its tall windows
and general aura of Victorian austerity.

establishment was presided over by the headmaster, Mr. Colthorpe, and it is at this point that the reader may find some variance with my reference to the loving, caring staff, for Mr. Colthorpe was no softy. He ruled over us with a rod of iron, and we all feared him. I have searched my mind for the best word to describe him and have decided to call him "authoritarian". Many of my contemporaries would undoubtedly have chosen more forthright words.

I was one of the few pupils on whom he never inflicted any form of physical punishment, but this was not necessarily because I was better behaved than the others. It was simply that there was one person of whom he was scared, and that was my mother. She held the strongest possible conviction that none of her boys would ever be guilty of a misdemeanour which justified caning. He knew that, if he dared carry out such an act, he would have some explaining to do, and he would never take the risk.

I remember one occasion when I came dangerously near to receiving his physical attention and it all came about because of Tommy Howard, a perpetually high-spirited classmate of mine. It was during a singing lesson from Miss Rump. Neither Tommy nor I was capable of producing musical notes in any form and we would hold our music in front of our faces so that it would not be seen that

45

we were not joining in. Tommy, however, was a great comic and he started saying funny things to make me laugh. Soon it became uncontrollable and Miss Rump could not fail to notice.

"Tommy! Bobby! Go to Mr. Colthorpe and tell him you've been misbehaving."

We immediately stopped laughing, for we knew that this meant "the cane". Tommy was not really bothered, for he had had more canings than hot dinners, but I was petrified. However, we had no choice but to present ourselves to the headmaster, who looked at us in disgust and told us to stand in front of his desk. He then lowered his head and continued with his paperwork. After what seemed like an eternity, he rose to his feet and I thought "Here it comes". But it was not so. Either he was trying to inflict mental torture on us or he wanted more time to decide whether it was worth risking my mother's wrath. Whichever it was, he suddenly left the room. Tommy giggled and said, "He's gone to get the big stick." This made me feel even worse.

By the time Mr. Colthorpe returned, the school bell had rung and all the other children had gone home. My state of apprehension was then so acute that I felt like pleading to be given the cane quickly in order to get it over. But it was not necessary. Mr. Colthorpe fixed us with an icy glare and said, "I shall let you go this time, but . . ." My brain was too numb to hear the end of his remark. We left the room in ungainly haste, me in a state of virtual collapse but Tommy happily declaring that, if it had not been for my mother, he would have had yet another caning to add to his ever-growing list.

My early years at the Council School had not brought me into contact with Mr. Colthorpe, for I started there at the age of five and was classed as a "mixed infant". It is true that he was head of the entire school, but he rarely gave his attention to us, preferring to leave us in the tender care of Miss Gow and Miss Dennis.

Miss Gow was, I suppose, a typical country schoolteacher. She was of uncertain age and there was nothing about her, either physically or academically, which would have made her stand out in a crowd. She was, however, a mother to us all, and her mode of discipline was based on love and respect rather than on fear.

She was assisted in her ministrations by Miss Dennis. Now, Miss Dennis was a different matter altogether. She was young and pretty, and when she smiled at me my legs turned to jelly. I loved Miss Dennis very much.

So it fell to these two ladies to give us our first introduction into an academic world, a task (or rather, perhaps, a vocation) which they carried out with never-failing care. They did not place too much emphasis on self-expression in those days. We were allowed to exhibit our own personalities and capabilities, but it was all done within the framework of the ordered routine of the day. We learned to read and write, to add and subtract and to do many other things, but above all we subconsciously absorbed the fact that all these things became simpler if tackled in an organised manner. Thus those two good ladies strived, with varying degrees of success, to develop in us that greatest of all possessions, an orderly mind. This training was to stand us in good stead when, a few years later, we would reach the age at which we would make the great leap forward into the hurly-burly of the "Senior Boys".

Although my years in the Infants' School were very happy, there was a period when, for reasons nobody could understand, I developed the habit of running away from school at some time during the day and going home. Even to this day I cannot think of any reason why I should have done it. Later on in my boyhood, and at a very different school, there was to come a time when I would dearly have loved to run away (and with good reason), but even a psychiatrist would have found it difficult to explain on this occasion. Whatever the reason, my mother began to dread the sound of my shuffling feet on the doorstep and my tearful voice through the letterbox saying, "Mummy, it's me". She would take me in and wipe away my tears. Then, off would come her apron and on would go her hat and coat and we would set off, hand-in-hand, back to school. There I would be welcomed back by Miss Gow or Miss Dennis, I would resume my place in class and my long-suffering mother would trudge back home to continue her work. I wish I knew why I did it!

The most exciting period of the year in the Infants' School was, of course, the few weeks before Christmas. Then it was that the increasing excitement of the coming celebration was heightened by the frantic activity which was necessary to make sure that everything would be ready on time. Little brushes were dipped into gluepots and applied to strips of paper, which then became transformed into multicoloured chains to decorate the classroom walls.

Christmas party time in the main schoolroom

Crepe paper was cut and, with a combination of dexterity and pins, became gaudy balls to hang from any available hook. Christmas cards, of an extreme simplicity matched only by their childish sincerity, were churned out ready for distribution to mothers and fathers, aunts and uncles, with an extra two being made in secret for Miss Gow and Miss Dennis.

But, above all, there was much work to be done in preparation for the annual school concert. This, of course, was no different from any other infants' concert, but to us it was an event of the greatest magnitude. The first time I took part in one of these productions was also the first time I had appeared on a public stage, and I was five years old. It was the conventional nativity story and I was to play the part of an owl. Looking back, I become aware that it was the only time I have ever known an owl to take part in a nativity play. I strongly suspect that the part was written in specially for me! Anyway, I was to be swathed in a piece of fur and put in my position behind a papier-mache tree, on the branch of which I was supposed to be perched. Then, as Joseph and Mary trudged on stage on their way to Bethlehem, I was to utter those immortal lines, "Tu-whit, to-whoo; tu-whit, to-whoo; tu-whit, to-whoo." I rehearsed with all the dedication of a National Theatre player and my debut went like a dream. Like every children's nativity play that has ever been presented, the show was a great success.

The Infants' Concert of the following year, though again voted a hit by the general public, was, for me, a personal disaster. This time we were performing a piece involving a selection of nursery rhyme characters and I was to play Humpty Dumpty. I was never under-weight as a child, but I still needed much help to create the image of the part, so our teachers set to work and made a most complicated cardboard frame which covered me from neck to ankles. The result was most impressive. There was this massive cardboard ostrich egg with my little head peeping out of the top and a pair of tiny feet underneath. I was unable to walk when I had the costume on, and Miss Dennis had to lift me on to the stage. I enjoyed that part most of all!

Well, all went well until the day of the Dress Rehearsal. I was feeling distinctly unwell that day and, by the time we had been taken to the Church Rooms to go through out parts, I was decidedly groggy. Miss Gow came to have a look at me and declared that I was suffering from "swollen glands", but that I would feel better tomorrow. Her diagnosis was only partly correct. By the morning my "swollen glands" had become mumps and I was feeling infinitely worse. Needless to say, the show went on without Humpty Dumpty and I was in the depths of despair.

A few days later, however, my world brightened considerably, this transformation being brought about by three things. Firstly, I didn't feel ill any more. Secondly, I had the most wonderful swollen face which I was proud to show to anybody who might show an interest. But thirdly, and most important of all, a young messenger brought to our house a package for me which contained some sweets and a letter from the sender. The letter, which I treasure to this day, read:

"Dear Bobby,
 This little box of sweets I hope you will enjoy. Perhaps it will make up a wee bit for your disappointment last week. Trust you will soon be well enough to return to school.
Your loving teacher,
F. Gow."
One fact which stands out above all others is that we children

were being brought up in a very caring community. When I look back upon those years the emotion which comes back most strongly is one of happiness and contentment. Furthermore, we were never bored. There was always so much to occupy our young minds that we never had time for boredom. When one bears in mind the fact, as borne out in my old school reports, that the average number of children in each class was consistently between 40 and 50, the success of that school was something to be proud of.

There was, however, one emotion which gradually began to assert itself, namely a sense of growing up. We had been in the Infants' School right from the start of our academic careers and now, as our last year there ran its course, our eyes were set on the "big boys' school" at the other side of the playground. We yearned to join the "big boys". This yearning was prompted, not just by the wish for seniority, but also by the fact that we would then be in an all-male community. In the Infants' School the sexes were mixed in together (I suppose the authorities thought we would never notice) but in the Senior School we became segregated.

I have never understood the reasoning behind this. It was certainly not dictated by the curriculum for, although we played football while the girls did needlework, everything else was the same. I can only assume that our elders feared we might regard the girls as sex objects and start getting naughty ideas. If this was the case I can only say how wrong they were. At the age of nine we were so grown up that we regarded girls merely as a nuisance and an interference in male activities. Hence, we could not wait to get away from them.

When school broke up that year for the harvest holiday, I left with a light heart. When the next term started, I would achieve my ambition. No longer would I be a "Mixed Infant". From now on I would be a "Senior Boy".

CHAPTER 6

Senior Boys

I well remember my great feeling of pride on the morning when I made my first entry into the "big boys' school". Looking back, I honestly believe that this represents one of the most significant steps in anyone's life, for it is inevitably the first great transition in one's progress towards the adult state.

My sense of pleasure stemmed not merely from the fact that I was saying goodbye to my infancy, but rather that I was acquiring a new lifestyle which only came with advancing years. First and foremost, there was the question of dress. No longer would I be required to wear the childish smock which, with the inevitable handkerchief attached by means of a safety pin, had been considered necessary to protect my clothing from the ravages of such things as chalk, crayon and modelling clay. There was no such thing as a school uniform, but henceforth I was able to appear in the ordinary clothing which marked me out as a "senior boy".

Then there was the fact that pencils, as material possessions, were to lose much of their significance. In the Infants' School most of our writing was done with pencils and the possession of any great number was, in fact, an indication of one's relative wealth. I was fortunate in that my father always wrote his "copy" with pencils and, when these became too short for comfort, he would gather them together and sharpen them for my use. Thus it was that I would sometimes arrive at school with my pencil box crammed with a dozen or more of the lovingly-prepared stubs and I was regarded as being rather well-to-do. From now on, however, we would be using pen and ink for most of our work. We were to learn all about thick strokes and thin ones and, most exciting of all, we were soon to be introduced to the intricacies of "joined-up writing".

The most significant change of all, however, was that henceforth, with the exception of music lessons from Miss Rump, we were to be taught exclusively by men. This caused certain problems in the early weeks when, through force of habit, we addressed a teacher as "Miss" instead of "Sir", but they understood our difficulty and treated us with forebearing during our period of adjustment.

It was about this time that I embarked upon my first love affair. I fell in love with the English language, and this love was to stay with me for the rest of my life. Without the distractions of wireless and television there was ample time for reading and I seized avidly upon everything I could find. Some of my reading matter at that time may not have been well-chosen, but at least it was varied. I read any printed word which presented itself and I have never lost that habit. Even today, my wife good-humouredly teases me over my tendency to read every word on the labels of sauce bottles and the like.

Although reading never gave me any great difficulty, there were one or two occasions in my early career when I encountered slight problems with words whose meanings were unknown to me. I recall, in particular, the days when, in unison, we recited the Lord's Prayer and I could never understand why we should implore God to "lead us not into Thames Station". Then there was the advertising hoarding which carried a poster proclaiming the virtues of a certain brand of coffee. There was a picture of a bottle of the product, together with the firm advice: "Don't be misled". Unfortunately, I mis-read this as "Don't be mizzled". I had no idea of what might happen if one allowed oneself to be mizzled, but I made a mental note that, if I wished to avoid such a fate in later life, I would be well-advised to drink Camp Coffee.

My greatest embarrassment, however, was caused by a certain delicacy which attracted my attention at our local sweet shop. I had seen it in the window in a little dish which bore the inscription: "Aniseed Balls, 2d per quarter". I decided that I would try them but, unfortunately, I failed to observe that there were two e's in the word aniseed. Thus my request to the shopkeeper was for "a ha'porth of anized balls, please, miss." I had no idea what the makers did to the balls to anize them, but I found them much to my liking and I continued to make a similar purchase every week. It was not until about the sixth week that, on hearing my request for "a ha'porth of anized balls, please, miss", the shopkeeper looked me in the eye and said, "You mean aniseed, don't you?" To say I was shocked would be an understatement. I was, in fact, grossly humiliated for, if she had known all along that I had mispronounced the word, why had she not had the decency to correct me earlier? My liking for aniseed balls disappeared at that very moment and they were, in fact, the last I ever purchased.

Such little upsets, however, failed to curb my enthusiasm for the written word and I went through the entire spectrum of children's publications which were available. The weekly comics started me off, but I soon tired of them because there were too many pictures and not enough words. I quickly graduated to such "big boys" papers as "The Gem" and "The Magnet" and was enthralled by the activities at Greyfriars School. My two favourites, however, were "The Children's Newspaper" and "The Boys' Own Paper". These two greatly differing publications held me enthralled for many hours each week and I was frequently on the newsagent's doorstep waiting for him to open his shop on the days when they were issued.

"The Children's Newspaper" was a true newspaper in every sense of the word. Edited by Arthur Mee, who had done such wonders with the "Children's Encyclopedia", it presented all the national and international news in a style considered suitable for young minds. I don't know whether I was a bit of a swot or whether it was the effect of the journalistic background at home, but I do know that I worked my way through every word of every column.

"The Boys' Own Paper" was a totally different concept. Lavishly produced on high-quality paper, it was copiously illustrated yet carried so many pages that there was sufficient reading matter to last for days. Tales of adventure in the outposts of the Empire and of prowess on the sporting fields of England rubbed shoulders with articles about every conceivable interest which was reckoned to appeal to the minds of healthy, developing British boyhood.

In spite of the wealth of weekly publications, however, my greatest joy came from books. Even before opening its pages, the feel of a well-produced book in my hands gave me a sensation of pleasure which remains with me to this day. I was never happier than when I could settle down in a quiet corner, open the pages of a book and experience the miracle of those printed words being transformed into images in my mind. Robinson Crusoe and the Swiss Family Robinson became real people; the explorer hacking his way through the African jungle had me by his side panting in anticipation as we fought our way forward together. How sad that modern children live in such a world of realism rather than one of imagination!

I suppose that it was inevitable, even at that early age, that I should develop the ambition to become a writer. As a small child I had watched my father laboriously writing out his reports in long-hand and, even before I learned that there were such things as letters and words, I tried to imitate his actions by drawing squiggly lines on sheets of paper. Every time he paused to think I did likewise and when his pencil returned to the paper mine copied his every action. As the beauty of the written word began to take a hold on me I wrote whenever I could. Stories and poems flowed from my pencil, as well as "newspaper articles" and even fictitious classified advertisements. Eventually I made my first entry into journalism – as editor of "The Busy B's Magazine".

The Busy B's were all schoolmates whose surnames began with the letter B and the magazine, limited to one copy, was laboriously printed out with one finger on an extremely ancient typewriter. I still have this unique first edition and it is interesting to note that it is an early example of two-colour printing in that the title was typed with the red part of the ribbon and the remainder with the blue part. The contents of the magazine are varied both in style and quality. Some are amusingly child-like while others appear so mature as to encourage certain doubts as to their originality. My contribution was a story entitled "The Redskin's Revenge", a stirring tale of dastardly deeds along the banks of the St. Lawrence River. Fred Buck supplied "A Sea Song", a poem which seems remarkably accomplished for a nine-year-old, whilst Rex Buckingham produced a spine-tingling science fiction epic under the title "The Hissing Death". I often wonder what happened to the Busy B's and all the other young lads with whom I shared so many boyhood experiences.

When I was ten years old, a significant figure came into my life in the form of a new teacher named Harry Allen. Mr. Allen was young, interesting and full of new ideas. I idolised him right from the start. His dark, slightly swarthy complexion and his black hair induced some of the boys to christen him "Rastus", but I would have none of it. To me he was always just "Mr. Allen". He represented something new to us, for he had an unbounded enthusiasm for his vocation and, with a mixture of encouragement and gentle nagging, he continually tried to draw the best out of each of us. I responded to his efforts and tried always to justify them. All the work I did for him was done with an ever-present urge to please. Then, in October 1930, I had my greatest chance of all to produce something which would repay his efforts.

He suddenly announced to the class that he was to hold a competition. All entrants had to write a "Scientific Essay" and the prize would be a book. His use of the word "essay" gave me a particular

54

thrill for, until then, the things we wrote had always been known as "compositions". "Essays" was a big boys' word! Anyway, I applied my mind to the challenge and decided to take as my theme the development of the aeroplane. Now, aeroplanes were not very numerous in the skies over North Walsham at that time and I knew very little about them. So there was only one thing to do – get out the Children's Encyclopedia. I knew that I must not copy what was written there, so I proceeded to read and memorise every section which had any bearing on aircraft. Then I set myself to the task of transmitting it to paper. Page followed page as I spent many a long hour writing and re-writing until, at last, I was satisfied. I was, in fact, more than satisfied. I was unforgiveably certain that no entry in the competition could in any way approach the quality of mine!

The day for handing in the entries duly arrived and then we awaited the result. I shall never forget that morning. My earlier confidence had begun to subside somewhat and nagging doubts had entered my mind. Eventually, Mr. Allen spoke. He started by saying how good all the entries had been and he seemed to go on and on. (Would he never get to the point?) He then reached the stage where he said that there were two entries which were so good that he had experienced the greatest difficulty in separating them. (My inner doubts suddenly took over complete control of my mind.) Then, after what seemed an age, he began to announce his decision. "The winner is . . ." Another lengthy pause followed and then – he spoke my name. My joy knew no bounds. I had won the prize but, above all, I had pleased Mr. Allen. The book, incidentally, was "Tarzan of the Apes", a strange choice, perhaps, in view of the subject matter of the essays, but one which still occupies a proud place on my shelves.

It was Mr. Allen who also introduced us to the world of real poetry. Prior to his arrival, our only encounters with this form of literature had been through nursery rhymes, limericks and, later on, some of the simpler poems, which we learned by heart and recited with a complete lack of feeling. Mr. Allen, however, had a great love of poetry, a love which he tried, with varying degrees of success, to communicate to us.

To help him in his task, he somehow managed to persuade Norfolk Education Committee to supply a set of copies of "A Treasury of Poetry". This was a very new publication, incorporating the work of poets as recent as Rupert Brooke and Wilfrid Owen (The memory of the War was obviously still fresh in the mind of the editor). Furthermore, it was the first time we had ever had books which had not been in the hands of previous occupants of our desks; even the feel of those untarnished volumes, smartly bound in green, was something to be savoured. To make the occasion even more special, there were enough copies for us to have one each. We sat two to a desk and normally, whatever the subject, we shared one text book between us. Having one's own personal copy gave us a sudden feeling of untold riches.

The selection of poems within was wide and varied. Some made an immediate impact on our minds while others were at first somewhat beyond our comprehension. Even the latter, however, sprang into life when Mr. Allen read them to us. The words rang clear and the images sprang from the pages as he went through every line with loving care.

We all soon had our own particular favourites. Billy Hicks and I were inseparable companions and we both rather liked James Hogg's "A Boy's Song":

> "Where the pools are bright and deep,
> Where the grey trout lies asleep,
> Up the river and over the lea,
> That's the way for Billy and me."

That last line was repeated at the end of every verse, and we felt that it could have been written specially for us. Many of the boys favoured "The Charge of the Light Brigade" or "The Burial of Sir John Moore after Corunna", for these pieces evoked the very spirit of our brave military forebears.

When Mr. Allen set us each the task of learning whichever poem we liked best, the result was varied in the extreme. Tommy Howard chose Robert Browning's little gem "Pippa's Song" after first making sure that it was the shortest one in the book. Rex Buckingham, the class swot, settled for Gray's Elegy but, as the complete poem ran to over thirty verses, he was allowed to confine his learning to the first six. As for me, I had no hesitation in going for Wordsworth's "Daffodils". The poem drew me to it like a magnet and, as I read the lines, the words became instant images in my mind as I wandered "lonely as a cloud" in the footsteps of the poet. Now, as I look back to those childhood days, I become increasingly aware that it was the unlikely combination of Harry Allen and William Wordsworth that was responsible for my introduction to the joys of poetry. Time and again I let my mind float back to that first book of poems, so smartly bound in green . . .

"And then my heart with pleasure fills
And dances with the daffodils."

Mr. Allen's teachings were directed principally at developing an appreciation of the written word, rather than a knowledge of the more technical aspects of writing. Such things as conjugation and syntax would come later, but for the present he was content to open the door and lead us into the world of literature.

There were, I remember, two pieces of advice which he regularly drove into our minds when we were striving to produce our own literary masterpieces. The first was that we should never waste words. "Never use two words when one will do", he would say. The second was that we should avoid repetition in our use of words. The wealth of words in the English vocabulary, he would tell us, was so great that it was always possible to find an alternative rather than to use the same one too frequently. To this end, he set about increasing our vocabulary by bringing to our notice long lists of words with similar meanings.

During the course of these studies, we found that we could also increase his vocabulary, for we used many words and phrases which were foreign to him. It is true that he was a Norfolk man, but he was from the City and we were country boys. There was not, at that time, the degree of integration which exists today, and the manner of speech of Norwich folk was totally different from that which prevailed in rural Norfolk. Not only were the two accents totally different, but there was also a vast range of words and phrases which were unique to the country dwellers. Some, of course, were common to both communities, but we frequently brought a smile to Mr. Allen's face when we produced some peculiarity of speech which he had not previously encountered.

He knew that "cushies" were sweets and a "mawther" was a young girl, for these words were in common usage. He was soon to learn, however, that we called a scarecrow a "mawkin" and a seesaw a "teeter-mer-torter", whilst, in the world of nature, an ant was a "pishimeer" and a snail a "dodman" or, more picturesquely, a "hodmadod". Furthermore, it was not merely our use of words which intrigued him, but also the phrases which we used in everyday conversation. A bad-tempered person was said to be "as short as a pie crust" whilst somebody who gave himself airs and graces was said to be "frimocking". I think the phrases he most liked were the ones we used to describe a simple-minded person. We would say that he "can't get no further than Wednesday" or, more forthrightly, "If his brains were dynamite, he wouldn't have enough to blow his cap off."

I often feel a tinge of sadness that so many of our descriptive old words and phrases have disappeared from everyday use. It seems that we are now so busy continually inventing new words that we forget the ones we already have. Even worse, perhaps, is the way in which the meaning of certain words is distorted to fit in with our modern lifestyle, and nowhere is this more apparent than with the word "gay". In my boyhood a gay was a coloured picture. We would say of a child with a book or comic: "He don't read it; he just look at the gays". Then there was the "gay" pony, which had a coat of contrasting colours.

No matter what one may feel about the old country vocabulary, I feel sure that Mr. Allen's education was broadened by his association with us. Even more true, however, is the fact that he left his mark on us. I, certainly, have much for which to thank him.

CHAPTER 7

Games and Pastimes

The generally uncomplicated nature of our lives in those early boy-hood years was largely reflected in the games and pastimes with which we filled our leisure moments. Many were seasonal in nature and some were dictated by the availability of natural materials. The one factor which was common to all, however, was their very simplicity, far removed from the electronic wizardry with which modern youth concerns itself.

One of the earliest to which we became addicted was the whipping top. This was a kind of inverted wooden cone which was set off by spinning it on its pointed base, after which the idea was to keep it in motion by means of deft flicks with a string whip. Even in our tenderest years we soon developed a high degree of skill and, before long, we progressed to the art of making the top travel long distances without losing its spinning motion. We soon became so adept at this that it became our normal practice to try and keep the top spinning all the way to school, a distance of something like a mile and a half. In spite of the unhelpful surface condition of some of the roads, we achieved this with increasing frequency.

Present-day roads would make the whipping top a much easier object to master but the volume of modern traffic makes it highly unlikely that the sport will ever be revived. At the peak of its popularity, however, the roads were peaceful places where the sight of a motor vehicle was almost a cause for comment. There were two Trojan vans in the district, one belonging to the baker and the other delivering Brooke Bond Tea, and occasionally one of them would come trundling along on its solid rubber tyres. Most of the traffic, however, was horse-drawn and the approach of Mr. Craske on his milk cart or Doctor Blewitt with his pony and trap could be perceived at a sufficiently early stage to enable one to manoeuvre one's top to the side of the road. There, hopefully, one would keep it spinning until the danger had passed. In any case, even the Trojans travelled at a somewhat modest pace. People were not in the habit of living their lives at breakneck speed in those days, though everything which had to be done somehow got done.

Early Motor Cars

My mother's brother Charles, a commercial traveller, was very proud
of his custom-built Chevrolet.

Doctor Blewitt caused quite a stir when he forsook his pony and trap for
a different kind of horse power.

The first tops we had were quite small objects, about two inches tall, usually found in one's Christmas stocking or amongst birthday presents. Soon, however, we yearned for something better and we would then set about making our own. A piece of suitable wood was cut from hedgerow or tree and, with the aid of a sharp penknife and an infinite degree of patience, each boy would try to outdo the others with his skill and artistry.

It was one such top, measuring all of five inches, which almost landed my brother Peter in a spot of trouble. He was proud of his creation and proceeded to whip it with all the strength at his command. Unfortunately for him, however, he landed a faulty stroke which caused the top to fly up into the air and take off over a nearby garden hedge. Almost immediately there was a crash and the sound of breaking glass. We hid behind the hedge until we were sure that nobody was coming out to investigate and then, when we deemed it safe, we looked over to see what calamity had befallen us. Peter's flying missile was easy to see, for it lay in solitary splendour in an otherwise empty greenhouse, right underneath the broken pane.

Nobody ever found out that Peter was responsible for the smashed glass, but he suffered daily punishment for his crime, for, every time we passed that garden, he could see his prized creation lying there and yet he knew that he would never get it back. To have gone to the house and requested permission to retrieve it would have been to admit his guilt. Thus, the supreme sacrifice had to be made.

Fortunately, the approach of autumn meant that our minds would soon be occupied with thoughts of other things, for it was then that certain trees would provide us with the raw materials necessary for some of our seasonal pastimes. The two trees which principally claimed our attention were the horse chestnut, which provided us with conkers, and the oak, from which we obtained ammunition for our popguns.

The best horse chestnut trees grew in the woods at Westwick, and this meant that Peter and I had a great advantage over most of the other boys. The woods belonged to Colonel Petre and were strictly private, but it so happened that our father was on friendly terms with the Colonel. Thus, whilst his gamekeepers kept other young trespassers at bay, we were allowed free access to gather up the autumnal harvest. This we did with great zeal, filling large sacks with sufficient conkers to last us through the season. We would struggle home with our precious load, and then we would begin the serious business of grading and drying the nuts.

At that time in Britain's social history, "conkers" was by no means just a trivial children's game. It was, in fact, a matter to be treated with the greatest seriousness and dedication, and we all applied ourselves to the task with appropriate zeal. We rejected a large proportion of our haul, for the slightest flaw or malformation could mean that the nut might let us down in the heat of battle. Then came the drying process, which also demanded great care and patience. Sometimes it was possible to carry this out more quickly in the oven, but this practice could be fraught with danger. The sudden application of heat could result in a brittle nut, and it was generally agreed that a slow, steady seasoning process was preferable. Some unscrupulous characters resorted to the practice of soaking the nuts in vinegar. This certainly produced a durable specimen which was extremely difficult to break, but the practice was regarded as being strictly illegal. Any boy who used such a nut without first admitting the treatment it had received ran the risk of becoming something of a social outcast.

The actual playing of the game was not merely a question of pitting the strength of one conker against another. During the course of the season, each nut built up a kind of pedigree, and the owner of such a specimen had the right to inspect that of a potential challenger before agreeing to go into battle. A nut which was being used for the first time was known as a "maiden", for it had no record on which its future performance could be assessed. When it achieved its first success it became a "oncer", then a "twicer", and so on. Furthermore, when one such nut beat another with a similar pedigree, it not only added one to its total, but also took over the record of its broken opponent. Thus, if a "fiver" beat a "sixer", it would then become a "twelver". Such specimens were highly regarded and would not be put into battle lightly or without a thorough assessment of the challenger's qualities. It was during contests of this kind that "conkers" came into its own as a spectator sport. Large groups of boys would gather to watch such a match and, as each side gave vocal support to its favourite, the excitement was felt as strongly amongst the onlookers as by the participants themselves. "Conkers" was a serious business, and the owner of a pedigree nut occupied a highly-regarded position in our boyhood fraternity.

Unlike the horse chestnut trees, the best oaks were to be found on the other side of the town, particularly in the area of Witton Heath and Bacton Wood. Throughout the summer we would make frequent trips to those plantations in order to assess the prospects for the crop of acorns which were so vital as ammunition for our popguns.

Just as the possession of a pedigree conker was a coveted status symbol, so the ownership of an efficient popgun was essential to any young lad who wished to maintain his position amongst his contemporaries. As with our earlier whipping tops, our first pop-guns were usually acquired as presents, but these manufactured products were regarded as little more than simple toys. They were very limited in both their range and the speed at which the missile could be projected. As we grew older, therefore, we found it necessary to make our own guns, and each of us worked frantically to produce a weapon with the kind of performance which would surpass those of our competitors.

The materials were readily available in the hedgerows, but careful selection was vital if the desired result was to be achieved. Elder was the best wood for the barrel and it was necessary to search for a straight branch which would give a finished product measuring some seven or eight inches in length. Then would begin the painstaking process of reaming out the pith to leave a cylinder with a calibre just wide enough to take a fairly tight-fitting acorn. For the handle we always used hazel, which had all the properties we needed. We would select a straight branch of approximately the same size as the barrel and then, leaving a handle of some three inches in length, we would begin laboriously carving the remainder to the required size to serve as the plunger. This had to be done with great accuracy for, whilst it must fit readily into the barrel, any degree of looseness would lessen the gun's efficiency by reducing the distance to which the acorn could be projected. It was a case of continually checking until one was satisfied, and it was only then that the weapon was put through the final process which ensured its maximum potency.

This involved moistening the tip of the plunger and rubbing it vigorously against a brick wall or similar rough surface to produce a brush-like effect. The purpose of this treatment was two-fold for, besides improving the seal inside the barrel and thus causing it to emit a louder bang when fired, it also induced a satisfying plopping sound when it was withdrawn prior to reloading.

It may seem strange that we did not regard our popguns as

offensive weapons, but certainly we did not use them to attack living creatures of any kind. Our skill as marksmen was judged solely by a combination of range and accuracy, and this could only be assessed by using inanimate objects. The acorns themselves were selected with great care but, unlike conkers, it was not possible to lay in a great store for future use. As they dried out they became less effective, and it was always desirable to use freshly-gathered specimens which still retained their fresh succulence.

There was one unfortunate side-effect which resulted from the efficiency of our hand-made popguns and this was the degree of physical effort needed to fire them. The toy versions we had used in younger days merely involved holding the barrel in the left hand and pushing in the plunger with the right. With our highly-developed weapons, however, it was necessary to hold the barrel with both hands and, by pushing the handle vigorously against one's body, exert the maximum possible pressure to send the missile flying on its way. There were many nights when I retired to my bed nursing a sorely inflamed abdomen which bore full testimony to the number of rounds I had fired off that day.

Although most of our boyhood pastimes were either seasonal in nature or, at best, transient in their appeal, there was one feature of our lives which continually held a fascination for us, and this was the cigarette card. Almost every packet of cigarettes included such a card and the producers of the various brands vied with each other in their efforts to attract the smoking public. Not only were the cards beautifully produced, but they also carried a wealth of information which filled our young minds with a knowledge extending over a wide range of subjects. All our sporting heroes were there, as well as such other attractions as "Outposts of Empire" and "Wonders of the World". There was a series of "Kings and Queens of England" which, though smacking slightly of school work, still needed to be collected. Wildlife featured strongly amongst the subject matter with collections of birds and animals, flowers and trees, together with more advanced topics such as "Nature's Struggle for Survival" and "A Wonderland of Insects". Much of my early knowledge of natural history came from the cigarette card.

The cards were usually produced in sets of fifty and we went to great lengths in our efforts to obtain a complete set of each particular subject. The sight of a man smoking in the street would encourage even the most timid among us to accost him with "Got any cards, mister?" while a discarded packet by the roadside would have us diving down to investigate its contents in the hope that the card would be nestling within. We all, naturally, carried any duplicates which had come our way, for use as "swops". It is a matter of great regret to me that I failed to keep any of the sets of cards which I so lovingly collected in those early years.

Quite apart from stimulating our collecting instincts, cigarette cards played another, and even more significant, part in our lives, for they also represented our major form of currency. Any purchases made in the local shops must, of course, be paid for out of our weekly pocket money but, in all business dealings between ourselves, it was cigarette cards which changed hands rather than coins. Furthermore, any particular boy's wealth was judged, not by his family background or the amount of his pocket money, but simply by the number of cigarette cards which he possessed. Thus it was that my brother Peter became indisputably the richest boy in North Walsham.

Peter, in those days, had a brilliant business mind and he was continually evolving new schemes in order to increase his wealth. Most of these schemes involved my cooperation as his assistant and I would be given a share of the profits in keeping with the part I had played although he, as organiser, naturally received the lion's share. We organised garden fetes, for which the entrance fee would be five cards. We set up sideshows of many kinds, which involved further payment of cards, and we also sold the lemonade which was produced in vast quantities by our mother. Then, when the paying public had left to return to their respective homes, Peter would sit at the table and, rather in the manner of a kind of childlike Scrooge, would count out the takings into bundles of a hundred, each bundle being securely bound with an elastic band.

I think our most successful events, however, were the horse-racing meetings which Peter organised. These took place in the churchyard and it is, of course, unnecessary to say that no horses ever took part. The entrants in each race were represented by the names of horses written on pieces of cardboard, and each boy was invited to stake a certain number of cigarette cards on which he thought would be the winner. When all the bets had been placed, the race would take place on a fairly straight stretch of the pathway which ran along in the shadow of the church. Peter, as starter, would throw the handful of cards as far as he could and I, in my capacity as Clerk of the Course, would be at the other end to declare the name of the winner. One boy would then be pleased with his winnings, but Peter would be happiest of all, for he always ensured that the prize money would never be more than fifty per cent of the stake money. I often think that, if he had carried his early business ability into adult life, he would have been a millionaire at a very young age.

Looking back on those early ventures into the gambling industry, I can only speculate upon the possible reaction of the Vicar if he had known to what purpose we were putting the grounds of his hallowed acre. In all our early activities, however, whether they involved whipping tops, popguns or any of the other accoutrements of our boyhood, only rarely did we come up against the heavy hand of authority. And I don't really feel that we did much harm to anybody.

CHAPTER 8

Travels With Billy

Billy Hicks was my best friend. I think, indeed, that I might well describe him as the best friend I have ever had. I say this with all due respect to the many people with whom I have since shared a bond of friendship, but the relationship between Billy and me was something quite unique. It was built on nothing more than a joy at being in each other's company. Neither of us had anything special to offer the other and neither expected anything save the mutual bond of going through life rather in the manner of two bodies with a single spirit. As I look back upon our very special relationship, my mind recalls the lines which Charles Lamb had written a hundred and fifty years earlier:

"Friend of my bosom, thou more than a brother,
Why wert not thou born in my father's dwelling?"

It would be wrong to suggest that Billy was ever more to me than any of my brothers, but ours was more than mere friendship. It was an association built on simple unstated love.

Billy and I came together when we were six years old and our friendship lasted for just five years until, because of my father's promotion to Head Office, our family pulled up its roots and began a new life in Norwich. Those five years, however, were crammed full of shared experiences and such a wealth of happiness as to make my early boyhood a period of utter joy and stability. This was something which could have been the lot of very few of my contemporaries, however, for conditions were hard in those depressed days of the late twenties. Unemployment was high and even those men who were fortunate enough to be in work received a rate of pay which was barely sufficient to cover essential household expenses. Furthermore, there were no welfare payments unless one happened to come under the protective umbrella of such friendly societies as the Foresters and Oddfellows. Luxuries were so few that even a tin of salmon for Sunday tea suggested that it was some special occasion.

Billy and I knew little of this, however, for we were both fortunate in having caring parents and, anyway, we found simple pleasures around every corner. We ranged far and wide in our travels and our lives were full of interest as we explored the countryside around us.

Billy's father was a builder and the yard adjoining their house was always packed with timber, bricks and the many other requisites of his trade. They had no garden as such, but Mr. Hicks did have a workshop, to which we managed to gain access for one brief period. There, Billy and I spent rainy days making ships which varied greatly in design but all shared the attribute of being completely unseaworthy. After a while, however, Mr. Hicks decided that he could no longer afford to subsidise us from his rapidly diminishing supplies of timber and nails, and we were banned from using the workshop.

One corner of the yard was given up to an enclosure where Billy kept a variety of domestic animals, mainly rabbits and chickens. The well-being of these creatures was a continual source of worry to Billy, and this was not helped by the constant practical jokes which his father's workmen were in the habit of playing on him. I recall in particular the time when a collection of young pullets had been installed and he waited impatiently for them to start laying. As the days went by with no sign of an egg, he became increasingly impatient until, one morning, he peered through the wire netting and saw the long-awaited vision of that first fawn-coloured, oval object nestling amongst the straw in the nesting box. His excitement knew no bounds as he darted inside to retrieve it, only to emerge a few seconds later with a look of utter despondency on his face. The object which he held in his hands was, in fact, not an egg, but a walnut which one of the workmen had placed there. One's memory can play strange tricks, but I have no recollection of those pullets ever starting to lay.

Billy's father also owned a meadow by the side of Kimberley Road, just a stone's throw from my home at "Woodland View". It extended over several acres and has more recently been submerged under a housing estate, but at that time it appeared to have no use whatever, except as a kind of cemetery for broken-down horse-drawn vehicles. There must have been at least thirty of them; gigs and traps, farm wagons and tumbrils, all lying there in varying stages of decay and eventual disintegration. Such a sight would have horrified the collector or conservationist of today, but it was merely that era's equivalent of the modern car breaker's yard.

In any case, those old vehicles were not entirely without friends, for Billy and I spent many a happy hour among them, driving mile after imaginary mile within their broken bodies. To us, however, they were not just pony traps and wagons, for we had a world of imagination within our minds. Thus, one would be a covered wagon in which we, as intrepid pioneers in the wastes of Canada, would drive our steeds madly onward into the interior. There would be frequent ambushes by Red Indians but, bringing our imaginary firearms into use, we would drive off all our attackers and come through unscathed. Another vehicle became a chariot, in which we took part in hectic races in ancient Rome. Our skill with whip and reins was such that even Ben Hur could have done no better than take second place. Just occasionally, though with much less enthusiasm, one of the old carts would become a tank which we would drive across the fields of Flanders. Whichever form our imaginary adventures took, we always finished the day with a flushed feeling of success, for we habitually overcame whatever dangers were encountered. Furthermore, those broken-down old relics continued to give us pleasure long after their working lives had ended.

Most of our pleasure, however, came from our expeditions further afield as we gradually explored the countryside which lay outside the town boundaries. We steadily expanded our territory, particularly as we grew older, and we soon had a long list of our favourite places. One of the first to find a place in our affections was the pond which lay out to the north-east by the side of the Blue Bell public house. This was a veritable haven of wildlife of all kinds. Reedmace, kingcup and water mint grew in profusion while bees and dragonflies hovered above. Most of all, however, it was the annual arrival of tadpoles which enthralled us. Once the frogs had spawned, we would make regular trips to watch developments and we would keep a constant vigil on the young fry until, eventually, the miniature new generation clambered out of the water and set off into a strange new world. Every year this process was repeated, for this was a very successful breeding place for all the local frogs. We had not, of course, inspected every stretch of similar water in the county, but Billy and I, nevertheless, had no hesitation in declaring this to be "the best tadpole pond in Norfolk". Sadly, more recent visits have given me cause to modify this high praise for, with its polluted water now filled with soft drink cans and plastic bags, there is little to attract any frog which possesses a modicum of self-respect.

Some distance further along on the road towards Bacton there is

The River Ant

The river bank above Bacton Wood Bridge where we shared our days
with sticklebacks and swallowtails.

Below the bridge, the limit of navigation for the old wherries which
travelled along the canal.

a hump-backed bridge which spans the River Ant, and it was at this spot that Billy and I probably spent our happiest times. It was here, almost a hundred years before, that the "navvies" from Bedfordshire had started cutting the seven-mile stretch of the North Walsham and Dilham Canal which was to bring earlier prosperity to North Walsham. When Billy and I found it, however, it had settled back into being just a quiet backwater where Nature had re-asserted itself and brought a return to peace and tranquillity. I am convinced, in fact, that it was our visits here which did as much as anything to stimulate the love of wildlife which was developing within me.

The river bank was carpeted in gold by masses of marsh marigolds, while the air above was filled with the fresh scent of meadowsweet. Ragged robin and valerian held out their nectar-filled blooms for visiting insects, whilst hemp agrimony and lady's smock offered an invitation to a multitude of small butterflies. Above all, however, there was milk parsley, and this meant swallowtail butterflies. We would lie back on the bank and watch these impressive creatures, sometimes as many as a dozen or more on the wing at one time, floating and weaving like miniature oriental kites, guided by unseen strings. Alas, the milk parsley has now all gone and, with it, the swallowtails.

There was, too, a wealth of active life within the water itself. Pond snails and leeches went about their business with almost imperceptible motion, in complete contrast to the feverish darting of the ever-active sticklebacks. Like most small boys, we went through the phase of catching sticklebacks and taking them home in a jam jar. This soon lost its attraction, however, for the little fish were much more interesting in their natural surroundings. By lying on our stomachs at the water's edge and almost submerging our faces, we could watch them going about their pre-nuptial activities, with the male using his home-made glue to fashion a nest. We gazed in fascination as he patiently inveigled the female within and then, having succeeded, maintained a constant watch until the young fry were ready to emerge. In later years we would read about such things in natural history books, but they were scenes which we had already witnessed at first hand.

In recent years there has been talk of restoring that little stretch of the Ant to its former glory. It would be nice to think that such a thing would be possible, though somehow I fear that nothing could bring back the magic which it once held for Billy and me.

In spite of our affection for that riverside spot, there were certain times during the year when we passed it by and headed off to the right towards Edingthorpe. There, in the shadow of Bacton Wood, was a farm which we were always allowed to visit, for it belonged to the father of one of our schoolmates. We spent many long days there, revelling in the constantly changing activities of the farming year and learning much about the lives of those who cultivated the land. I fear, however, that such knowledge as we acquired would stand us in very poor stead today, for it was a time when men and horses still reigned supreme in the fields of Norfolk. The reaper/binder had arrived and there was even a rumour that a farmer in another part of the county had brought into use the first combine harvester, but hands and horses were still the major factors in the life of Heath Farm.

There was, however, the threshing machine, and it was this great leviathan which we had been invited to see in action on our very first visit. The threshing gang went round the countryside with all their equipment, travelling from farm to farm to deal with the stacks of corn which had stood in field or rickyard since the previous August. Billy and I arrived early, but only just in time to see the stately procession of vehicles swing round the far corner and start the final lap of its journey. Our friend Jack was there to meet us, but first he had to obey his mother's command to go indoors and shut all the windows, while she herself dashed out to collect her washing from the line and take it inside under cover. We were soon to appreciate the wisdom of these actions.

Eventually, the steady cavalcade reached the gate and turned into the yard. First came the steam engine, its tall chimney belching a cloud of black smoke as it took up its required position. Then followed the threshing drum, hung around with the bicycles which the men always took with them. Finally there came the tall elevator which would carry the straw away from the drum to the top of the new stack which was to be built. It all happened with great precision and at a stately pace which gave no indication of the feverish fury which was soon to envelop the scene.

The change took place the very second that the engineer set his great drive belts in action. Black smoke billowed through the yard, chaff and dust blew around in heavy clouds and every single man sprang into furious action. Two or three stood on top of the corn stack with their pitchforks at all angles as they hurled the sheaves down to the most trusted member of the gang, the "feeder". He, huddled and squat inside the top of the thresher itself, cut the binding straw of each sheaf and fed it almost lovingly into the shaking jaws of the thresher. Out of the other end came the threshed straw to be carried up the elevator to where two or three other men were meticulously building the new stack. From a chute at the other side came the grain, shiny and clean, to be collected into sacks and weighed by the farmer and his helpers.

All the while the engineer, ever busy with oil can or coal shovel, watched over his pulsating machine. He always claimed that he was the most important member of the team. Our admiration, however, went to the "feeder", poised precariously over that frantically churning drum, for we felt certain that, if he lost his balance, he would most certainly come out of the other end as a bag of corn.

Compared with the rumbustiousness of the threshing yard, the harvest field was almost a haven of peace, for the only concession to technological development was the reaper/binder. This implement had, of course, spelt the end for the scytheman, but even he was needed to deal with those areas of corn which, having been flattened by heavy rain, were beyond the capabilities of the binder. There was also the field margin where, with sickle and crooked stick, men would prepare a path for the reaper and his team.

Nowadays, of course, a mere handful of men with their mechanical giants can reduce a vast acreage to naked stubble with unbelievable speed. In those more peaceful days, however, the harvest field drew all men to it, together with as many horses as could be mustered. Ploughboy and cowman, carter and shepherd were all there, together with the women and children who would help to stook the sheaves. As the sheaves of corn, each neatly tied around the middle, fell from the binder, they were gathered together and stood on end in groups to dry in the warmth of the sun. This was done, not in any kind of haphazard manner, but strictly in accordance with a routine which had been evolved over the years. Thus, there were always eight sheaves of wheat or barley to a stook, but fewer of oats, lest they should "heat".

As Billy and I helped to build up that traditional scene of the August landscape, we felt a glow of satisfaction at the part we were playing in bringing in the golden harvest. As the day wore on, however, our joy was to be broken by intermittent bouts of sadness, for there was tragedy within that ever-reducing square of standing grain. All day long little hearts were beating fast as the rabbits

Our first view of the threshing cavalcade as it arrived at the farm.

Threshing in full swing in the rickyard.

Man and horse still reigned supreme in the fields of Norfolk.

The harvest field was a haven of comparative peace.

75

cowered from the pounding hooves and the slashing reaper blades. Eventually would come the break for freedom, and they were not to know that there were men out in the open ground, waiting with guns. There would be a frantic leap out over the stubble; the sound of gunfire would ring out; and then there was just a wriggle, and silence. We boys were supposed to drive the rabbits towards the guns, but Billy and I would have no part in it. Every now and again, one of the terrified creatures would bolt from the standing corn and, unseen by the guns, reach the safety of the woodland. Whenever this happened, our hearts would pound with pleasure. Much as we loved the land, there were certain aspects of farming life with which Billy and I found great difficulty in coming to terms.

Of all my early harvest recollections, the one which stands out most vividly in my memory is the proud day when I was made the "howdgee boy". It was the time of carting corn to wherever the stack was to be built, either in the rickyard or in the corner of the field, and it was all done with horse-drawn vehicles. Now, it should be explained that there were four basic commands which were used to control horses. Turning to the right was achieved by the cry of "Cumhether", whilst "Capper" was for turning left. More importantly, starting and stopping were brought about by the commands "Giddup" and "Howdgee" (hold-ye). In order that the men could concentrate on loading the wagons, it was the custom for one of the bigger boys to control the horse, and to do this satisfactorily meant sitting on the horse's back.

Prior to this day I had never ridden on any animal, not even a seaside donkey. Furthermore, although I was probably ten or eleven years old and thus classed as a "big boy", that horse was gigantic. Thus, when the carter decreed that it was my turn to be "howdgee boy", my emotions were a mixture of pride and panic. I had no time to dwell on the matter, however, for, almost immediately, his strong arms gathered me up and, with one great swing, deposited me on the animal's back. As I looked down, I became even more aware of the giddy height at which I was perched. Even worse, however, was the realisation that the animal, quite apart from being tall, was also very, very broad. As I stretched my legs around its great girth I felt a pain which suggested that my entire body would split up the middle. Furthermore, any effort to adjust my position was fraught with danger, for there was, naturally, no saddle, but merely a sack slung over the animal's back.

Nevertheless, my feeling of pride ensured that I soon forgot my physical discomfort and, throughout that afternoon, I carried out my duties with impeccable skill. I will never know how much of my success was self-achieved and how much was attributable to the horse, for he had seen it all before and I was a mere beginner. There is, however, one thing of which I am certain and that is that, as he swung me onto the horse's back, that carter made a small boy very happy.

In our five years of friendship, I suppose nothing really exciting or newsworthy every happened to Billy and me. As we ranged far and wide in our own little world, however, we shared a wealth of experiences which made our relationship something special. When, in 1931, we came to the parting of the ways, Billy wrote in my autograph book:
"Remembrance is a golden chain
Which links true friends together,
And if we do not break this chain
We remain true friends for ever."
Sadly, we allowed the chain to break.

More recently, my efforts to trace him have brought no success. Similar attempts in relation to others amongst my boyhood friends almost unfailingly brought sadness when I found that they had gone away to war in 1939 and had not returned. I pray that this fate did not befall Billy. If it did and he now lies in some foreign field, I would prefer not to know. Much better, I feel, to remember him lying on the river bank with swallowtails fluttering above or crouched over the water's edge watching the stickleback painstakingly building its nest.

CHAPTER 9
Night Life

Like most similar country towns, North Walsham in the twenties was a rather sleepy little place and there was not much in the way of organised activities to occupy the minds of the local youngsters. There were the weekly meetings of the cubs and scouts which attracted some of us but, for the most part, we made our own entertainment. Professional offerings were not only very few and far between but also mediocre in quality when compared with today's highly sophisticated attractions. Nevertheless, we seized every opportunity which presented itself and we were oblivious to any shortcomings as we made the most of what was offered.

The Picturedrome was our mecca on most Saturday evenings, for it was the only cinema in the area. The entertainment was modest when judged by present-day standards for this was before the arrival of "talkies" and, besides being silent, the films were all in black and white. This, however, did nothing to lessen our enjoyment, for we had never known anything different. Furthermore, for an admission charge of one penny (or threepence for the front row) we could enjoy something like two hours of fantasy and excitement.

Long before the show was due to begin we would wend our way towards King's Arms Street with our precious coppers clasped in our hands. The unprepossessing exterior of the building gave little indication of what was to be found within but, once inside, we were introduced to another world far removed from our normal daily life. I am not sure whether our mother really approved of our mixing with all the rough boys of the neighbourhood in the cheap seats for, on the odd occasion when her purse would stretch to it, she would give us sufficient money to sit in the front row. I well recall one evening when, as we made our way along Kimberley Road, Peter was playing with the sixpenny piece which she had provided and he managed to drop it in the long grass by the roadside. A lengthy search in the darkness failed to reveal it and we had no choice but to return home. The loss of such a coin was a heavy blow, but our mother immediately searched in her purse so that we would not be disappointed. This time, however, it was only two coppers which she could spare, so we had to be satisfied with the cheaper seats. To be perfectly honest, we were much happier in the "pennies".

The Picturedrome was owned and staffed by Mr. and Mrs. Trollope and they ran it in a most disciplined and systematic manner. Before the show began, Mrs. Trollope sat in the admission kiosk to receive our pennies while her husband was down in the hall (I hesitate to call it an "auditorium"), ushering us to our seats and making sure that we stayed in them and behaved in an orderly manner. When the full audience had assembled, the doors were locked and, after a final admonition to us to behave ourselves, Mr. Trollope went up into his projection box. Mrs. Trollope then mounted the stage and sat at the piano, where she would proceed to provide the show with a suitably varied musical accompaniment. Her skill at switching from one melody to another to suit the changing moods represented on the screen must have been considerable, although we were too young to appreciate her wizardry at the time. Her music was an integral part of the performance and we accepted it as such.

The first half of each week's show was usually fairly serious in character and then, after a short pause while Mr. Trollope changed reels, we were regaled with comedies. We were always ready to laugh and we liked the comedies best of all. Mr. Trollope knew this only too well and on many occasions, if we were becoming a trifle too boisterous for his liking, he would stop the film and silence us with the threat: "If you boys don't behave I shan't put the comic on!" This instantly achieved its aim and the remainder of the programme was completed with a reasonable degree of order.

Strangely enough, the only occasion on which I have been reduced to tears by an actor's performance was within the walls of the Picturedrome. I cannot remember the name of either the film or the performer, but the plot concerned the life of a poor little orphan boy who was reduced to begging in the street. Accompanied by his scruffy, but faithful, mongrel dog, he would play his violin in all weathers and hope for charity from passers-by. It was all very sad, and this sadness reached its peak in one particular scene when a policeman arrived and, taking the dog from the boy, threatened the young lad with prison if he continued begging. The dog struggled to escape from its captor, the little boy's eyes began to fill with tears – and I dissolved into a fit of uncontrollable sobbing. Later, after I had recovered, I vowed that it was the best film I had ever seen!

However, as I said, it was the comedies which gave us the greatest pleasure. Harold Lloyd, Fatty Arbuckle, Our Gang and the Keystone Cops – we loved them all and the Picturedrome gave them to us in full measure. Some years later, a smart new cinema was built in another part of the town, with a large screen and talking pictures. We went once or twice, but it was never quite the same.

Once a year the travelling fair arrived in Town and flaunted its attractions on the Station Meadow. We always knew of its impending arrival well in advance for, long before the great day, coloured stickers suddenly appeared on telegraph poles and trees throughout the area informing the local populace of the thrills and mysteries which were soon to be made available to them.

We were glad of this advance notice, for it gave us time to save our pennies in readiness for the great event. You see, we knew that our mother didn't really approve of our attendance at the fair. She never actually forbade us to go, but she made it clear that she didn't consider it fitting for her boys to mix in such rough company. Thus, we could not expect her to subsidise our visit and the result was a period of abstinence to enable us to guard our precious coppers. The aniseed balls and sherbet fountains stayed unpurchased on the sweet shop shelves and Mr. Jeary's Vantas drink (our favourite beverage) remained untapped upon his counter. By this means, my brother Peter and I might possibly have as much as a shilling between us by the time the fair arrived.

The entrance to Station Meadow was through a perfectly normal wooden farm gate. For 364 days of the year this gate was such a mundane object that it rated not a second glance as we passed it on our way to and from school. On the night of the fair, however, a transformation took place. We always waited until dusk before making our entrance, for everything seemed so much more exciting at that time of the day. Then, as we passed under the railway bridge, the full spectacle hit us with the force of a cannonball. Over the gateway there had been erected an arch, from which a festoon of coloured lights blazed out a gaudy welcome. From all corners of the meadow similar lights flickered and shone as the mechanical music of the merry-go-round struck joy into our hearts. Mingling in with this wondrous sound were the voices of the barkers, stridently vying with each other for our custom, together with the excited chatter of their prospective patrons. As we walked through the entrance, that wooden gate was no longer the familiar object of yesterday. It had become the beckoning hallway into a veritable Aladdin's Cave of thrills and excitement.

We spent a long time exploring the magic scene before spending any of our money. It was well known to us that, like so many pleasures of life, the best part was the anticipation. We studied every ride and stall. We passed by the popcorn man and we positively shunned the lady selling rock. Our mother would never allow us to eat fairground rock, which she believed to be unhygienic. She made sure we never bought it by telling us that, when on the road, the fairground travellers kept it under their bed! As a result, never in my life have I tasted fairground rock.

The greatest fascination for us lay in the wealth of booths which, spread all around the meadow, housed a wide variety of freaks and oddities. There was, of course, always a Bearded Lady, but we didn't want to see her. There was another lady who was said to be "half girl and half fish". The very thought of such a creature intrigued us and we might well have succumbed had it not been for the presence of a nearby tent which housed an even greater attraction. We stood before it and, as the barker rang his bell and expounded upon the mystery which was to be found within, we read the notice which, in huge letters, proclaimed it to be "THE BIGGEST RAT IN THE WORLD". Peter and I looked at each other and, as our eyes met, we knew that this was something not to be missed. The entrance fee was twopence, but we knew that it would be well worth it. We parted with our coppers and entered the tent.

It was gloomy inside but, as our eyes became slowly accustomed to the darkness, we could make out the shape of a wire cage over which a somewhat soiled piece of cloth had been hung. With the other patrons, we waited impatiently for the creature to be revealed. Eventually, the great moment arrived and, with a flourish, the barker removed the cloth. A gasp went through the little crowd of onlookers. We couldn't believe what we saw. There, before us, was this great creature, as large as a medium-sized dog, with a two-foot long body bearing an eighteen-inch tail. Furthermore, for good measure, it possessed a huge head and a large humped back, together with webbed hind feet. Its incisor teeth were of a vivid orange hue and its whiskers longer than anything we had ever seen. We stood dumbfounded as we took in every detail of this mammoth rat. Then, as quickly as it had begun, the show was over and we shuffled outside, chattering excitedly about the strange creature. We both agreed that our money had been well spent.

It was to be many years before I realised that the animal at which we had gazed that night was not a rat but, in fact, a coypu.

My first introduction to the live theatre came with the arrival in Town of a travelling concert party under the name of "Streamers". We had no advance warning of their impending arrival; the first indication we received was from a man who stood outside the school as we went in on that particular morning. He handed us gaily-coloured leaflets informing us that the Company would be giving two performances in the Salvation Army Hall that very day at 4.15 and 7 o'clock. Everybody would be welcome to attend and the admission charge was fourpence for adults and twopence for children.

Peter and I could hardly contain our excitement that morning, and the lessons seemed to drag on and on until eventually the bell rang for our dinner break. He, of course, was in a higher class than me, but we met up at the school gate and ran all the way home to tell our mother and persuade her to allow us to go to the show. She listened to our excited chatter and then, after rummaging through her purse, produced four pennies. These she put into Peter's pocket for safe keeping, for it would be necessary for us to go straight from school to the Hall in order that we might get good seats.

Soon after 4 o'clock the Hall was full of excited, chattering children waiting for the concert to begin. Eventually, all the lights except the one on the stage were switched off and, for the next hour, we were all in another world. The performance was somewhat basic and unsophisticated, but the artistes held us entranced, for we had never seen anything like it before.

There was a man playing the piano and we marvelled at the fact that he had no music. We decided that he was even cleverer than Mrs. Trollope at the Picturedrome. There were two ladies who sang solos and duets and also danced to the accompaniment of the pianist. They seemed to wear different dresses for each item, and to our young minds it was all a wonderland of colour and excitement. Our favourite, however, was Harry Carr, a comic who was the agreed star of the show. He was very much in the mould of the typical North Country comedian and he held us under his spell with a succession of funny stories the like of which we had never heard before.

The high spot of his act obviously owed much to the world of pantomime and to Widow Twankey in particular. We had never seen a pantomime and we knew nothing of the comical widow, but he had presumably played the part in many Christmas shows, for there he was, dressed in the voluminous skirts, striped stockings and baggy knickers which are the trade mark of the character. Thus attired, he regaled us with continual comical quips as he worked away at his ironing board. Eventually, he came to the climax of his act when, after starting an argument with a member of the audience, he suddenly threw his flat iron vigorously out into the hall in the direction of the startled person. Needless to say, the sight of the approaching missile caused everybody in the near vicinity to dive frantically for cover, only to rise again in confusion when they realised that the flat iron, being attached to a length of elastic cord, had sprung back into Widow Twankey's hand. The effect was dramatic and the atmosphere electric, for North Walsham had seen nothing like this.

Peter and I made our way home to tea in a state of great excitement, for we had so much to report. On arrival, we were met by our mother, who told me that my friend Billy Hicks had called round. His mother had given him fourpence so that he and I could go to the evening performance. Not wishing to disappoint Billy, my mother made no mention of the fact that I had already seen the show. I also kept the secret as Billy and I later made our way to the Salvation Army Hall, but I had already conceived a plan with which to surprise him. On entering the Hall, I would manoeuvre him over to the area at which Widow Twankey's flat iron would be directed. Then, at the moment when the missile came our way, I, knowing the secret, would be the only one to remain sitting upright. Billy could not fail to be impressed by my courage.

Well, the performance began and I enjoyed it even more than I had in the afternoon, probably because of my excited anticipation of the trick I was to play. Eventually, Harry Carr started his scene at the ironing board and then, after arguing with a member of the audience, he sent the iron hurtling on its way. Billy dived for cover. All the other people around him dived for cover. And me? I am afraid my courage failed me at the last moment, and there I was, diving for cover with the rest of them.

CHAPTER 10

Miss Smith

I suppose it was inevitable that, in my formative years, most of my time would be spent under female influence, for it was an age which decreed that man was the provider while woman was the protector of offspring. I believe this tradition still survives in some quarters although the passage of the years has seen the demarcation line become more and more blurred. In the first quarter of this century, however, that tenet of life was fairly strictly adhered to, and certainly my early years were under largely feminine control.

In the home it was our mother who exercised the main guiding influence and, when I ventured forth each day to school, there I would spend long hours of every day under the protective wings of an all-female staff. Modern theorists might possibly claim that such an upbringing was destined to produce a race of cissies, but I can assure them that such was definitely not the case. We learned the virtue of deference to all our elders and betters, irrespective of sex, but at no time was it allowed to cloud our own natural male person-alities. Our female mentors seemed to have an instinctive flair for discovering the latent talents of their charges, something which was not always apparent when one was later to become enshrouded in the all-male bastion of a boys' grammar school.

Quite apart from home and school, there was yet another woman who possessed that same flair for encouraging the proper development of young male minds. That person was Miss Smith, our cubmistress. We loved and respected her, and I am sure the effects of her influence made their mark on many a young lad who passed through her hands.

By day, Miss Smith was immersed in a world of high finance, for she was the manager of North Walsham Penny Bank. I had an account with her, but I fear it did little to maintain the Bank's solvency, for my pocket money was only threepence per week. I still have my bank book and it is interesting to note that the largest deposits, sometimes as much as half-a-crown, were always on June 19th – obviously birthday money! The book also indicates that I have a credit balance which has been there since 1932. It must have earned quite a bit of interest since then, but, sadly, it is many years since the North Walsham Penny Bank faded into the shadows of history.

Although she was my early financial adviser, my main reason for remembering Miss Smith is because of her leadership of the 1st North Walsham Wolf Cubs. She led the pack with a dedication and enthusiasm which transmitted itself to the boys and made "Cub Night" something which we all regarded as one of the high spots of our week. Immediately after tea on Tuesdays we would don our uniforms and make for the Cub Hut which stood in the corner of a field by the railway embankment on the edge of Town. It was a flimsy wooden building with a corrugated iron roof, but to the two dozen or so boys in the pack it represented a weekly trip to some kind of promised land. There Miss Smith would take us through our DYBs and DOBs, read us excerpts from Rudyard Kipling and generally inculcate in us the spirit of Lord Baden Powell. We would gather in a circle and sing camp songs, although we never actually went to Camp, and Miss Smith would proudly hold the totem pole. This pole, surmounted by a carved effigy of a wolf's head, was a bit of a mystery to us, but we knew it was something to be revered, rather like the regimental colours carried into battle by fighting soldiers of an earlier day. Then we would vote amongst ourselves to decide who was the best boy in the pack, and the winner would receive "The Cup". This was the tiniest trophy one could imagine, but it was the greatest honour the pack could confer on one of its members.

The pack was divided into sixes, each of which was led by a "sixer" and a "seconder". These were easily identifiable, for the former was privileged to wear two bands of yellow ribbon around one arm while the latter had a single band. I carried neither of these badges of office, for I was merely a "tenderfoot". Furthermore, I was not even permitted to wear a woggle to keep my kerchief in place. Until I had finished my tenderfoot stage I had to manage by knotting it under my chin. I was, in fact, the youngest member of the pack and very much in the shadow of my brother Peter, who led his six with great vigour.

In view of my love for Miss Smith and the Cubs, it seems incongruous that they should have been the central figures in one of the most deplorable incidents in my life and one which still fills me with a strong feeling of remorse. I had not yet reached my eighth birthday and I suppose that I could claim that I was led astray, but it was an incident which began with misplaced loyalty and finished with a degree of shame which I, at such a tender age, found great difficulty in bearing.

Peter and I were friendly with two other brothers of similar ages to ourselves, namely Kenny and Douglas Brown, who were also cubs. On the evening in question, we had enjoyed the usual routine of Cub Night and had come to the end of our activities. Miss Smith was about to dismiss us when she turned to Peter and Kenny and told them that, because of their bad behaviour, she did not wish them to attend on the following Tuesday. I was unaware that they had misbehaved, but apparently Miss Smith had seen something which had escaped my eyes.

On the way home, the two older boys discussed the situation and tried to devise a plan. To tell their mothers that they were not allowed to attend the next Cub Night would have meant giving an explanation, and neither boy was prepared to face the wrath which such a confession would bring down upon them. Thus the plan was hatched. They would say nothing but, at the normal time, they would don their uniforms and set off to the hut in the usual way. Then, when the meeting was over, they would make their way home and nobody would suspect a thing.

It was at this point that my part in the drama began, for Douglas and I decided that, if our brothers were not going to Cubs, then nor were we! We, also, would put on our uniforms next Tuesday and act exactly as though it had been a normal Cub Night. What I did not know at that time was that my loyalty to my brother was to end eventually in a tangled web of deceit.

Anyway, the following Tuesday arrived and then, after tea, we put on our Cub uniforms and set off in a casual manner for the Cub Hut. On the way we met up with Kenny and Douglas Brown and we decided that we would climb the railway embankment so that we could keep an eye on events down below. By that means, we would know when the pack dispersed and we could then make our way home.

We climbed the embankment and sat down. We saw Miss Smith arrive and we saw the cubs turning up in little groups until the complete pack had assembled. We saw the door being closed. We heard silence fall upon the hut. Then we heard the Dybbing and Dobbing, and we heard the muffled voice of Miss Smith reading from Rudyard Kipling. Eventually all was quiet. Still we sat. When we had been inside the hut, the time had always seemed to fly. Now, sitting on that embankment, time stood still. It seemed an eternity. We were bored.

Eventually, Kenny picked up a small stone and threw it into the air. Our eyes followed it as it flew above the meadow and landed on the roof of the hut. It was at this point that the silence was shattered as the stone rattled down the corrugated iron and fell to the ground. There was a pause, and then another stone flew through the air, hit its target and rattled its way downwards. Then there was another, and another. Soon the air was filled with the raucous rattle of a multitude of pebbles scraping their discordant route across the rusty metal and falling in a heap below.

Then, with startling suddenness, the noise ceased as the door of the hut opened and a young cub's voice called out, "Bobby, Miss Smith wants you." I froze. Why should she want just me when there were four of us? But the boy's voice continued: "You've won The Cup." My brain was a tangle of mixed emotions. I was thrilled to have won The Cup, but how could I claim to be the best boy in the pack when I had spent the evening with this gang of revolutionaries? Kenny Brown leaned across. "Go and get it," he said. "It will be proof that you've been to Cubs." I yielded. I went down the embankment and across into the hut. Miss Smith said not a word as she gave me the trophy. I thanked her, turned and made my way out again.

The rest of the evening was incident-free. I think my mother was pleased that I had won The Cup. She gave it pride of place on the mantelpiece.

The next day, Peter and I went to school as usual and then, at 12 o'clock, we went home to dinner. There were no school meals in those days, so we made the journey home, even though it was a mile and a half each way. The events of the previous evening had already faded in our memories, but soon they were to be brought back into focus with a frightening jolt. Our mother met us at the door, her face white and lined and bearing an expression of such severity as I had never seen on it before. She had had a visit from Miss Smith and the sickening truth about our escapade had been revealed.

My mother did not punish us, but she demanded an explanation. She lectured us. She harangued us. But, worst of all, she made it abundantly clear that we had let her down and we had let Miss Smith down. That was punishment enough. But she did make one demand – I was to take The Cup back to Miss Smith that very afternoon and tell her I was not a fit person to hold it. I did as I was told, and Miss Smith was so kind that I burst into an uncontrollable flood of tears.

The 1st North Walsham Wolf Cubs

The full pack, with Miss Smith proudly holding the totem pole. I am second from the left in the middle row, with Peter standing behind me.

The Cubs' football team. Peter, as captain, holds the ball while I sit cross-legged at his feet.

Nothing was ever said about the incident after that. Miss Smith forgave and forgot. My mother forgave and forgot. Somehow, I have never been able to forget.

From that day onwards, however, my career as a Cub progressed steadily and I eventually reached a high position in the pack. I became a seconder and then – joy of joys – a sixer. I was also destined to lead our football team in matches against other similar groups, so perhaps I redeemed myself in the end. Certainly Miss Smith held me in high regard, a fact which is recorded for posterity by an inscription in my childhood autograph book which is headed: "To a good sixer." I never missed another Cub Night and I was always on parade to lead my six whenever our services were required. The Armistice Day Parade, the Town Carnival, the special Assembly to mark the 20th anniversary of King George's Coronation – always the 1st North Walsham Wolf Cubs were there, marching in style with the best the town could muster.

As I have said, we never went away to Camp, but there was one event which was easily the high spot of one particular year. Miss Smith's brother was a farmer a few miles from Town and we were to spend one Saturday there as his guests. Transport was a problem, but he soon solved it by sending one of his tumbrils for us. I suppose the sight of a farm cart carrying a score of excited young boys off into the countryside would cause a few heads to turn nowadays, but at that time it was commonplace, for that was how we went on our Sunday School treats and other outings.

We were all country lads but, even so, a day on a farm with the actual farmer was a great excitement. We helped to muck out the pigs and we watched the cows being milked (it was all done by hand at that time). We engaged in a multitude of activities, and then it was time to go indoors for high tea. There we were, in that vast kitchen, with dishes of steaming sausage and mash nestling in our laps. Our excitement dulled our sense of tiredness until it was time to go home, and then we tumbled out into the yard and climbed up onto the tumbril. By that time darkness was falling and two flickering lamps struggled to light our way through the country lanes. We lay in a tangled heap, too tired to move but with eager eyes picking out the strange forms of the ever-changing shadows as we ambled past hedgerow and ditch. Then we were in North Walsham. We showered thanks on our host and then dispersed in all directions to our homes, declaring in unison that it had been the best day we had ever had.

CHAPTER 11

The Big City

One of the great experiences of my early boyhood was the occasional visit to Norwich. Such trips were very few and far between, for few people did much travelling in those days. The traders of North Walsham were fully capable of supplying most of our everyday requirements and it usually needed some special set of circumstances to induce a trip to "the city". There might be times when my father's presence was required at the Press office in London Street and, if I was lucky, he would take me with him. For the most part, however, I went in company with my mother, who made the journey perhaps two or three times a year.

Most of our trips were made by train, for it was not until later years that the first motor coach travelled along that route. The journey took about forty minutes, but it always seemed to be over in far less time than that, for there was so much to be seen from the big carriage windows. The scene was ever-changing as the train chugged and puffed its way through Worstead and Wroxham, Salhouse and Whitlingham, and then on to the very edge of Norwich itself. Thorpe Station was somewhat frightening, for it was full of steaming trains and hurrying people, but my excitement really began when we emerged from the station yard to find the big city spread out before us.

We could well have boarded a tram at this point, for there was a constant procession of these magnificent vehicles clanging their way through the city streets. This, however, was not part of my mother's plan; the tram ride was a treat reserved for later on. Thus, we made our way over Foundry Bridge with that great river flowing beneath, and started along Prince of Wales Road. This was a magnificent thoroughfare at that time and no visitor could have wished for a more impressive and welcoming entrance to the city. Up and away it went in a wide, sweeping curve, with those tall buildings, so lovingly constructed in a more peaceful age, gazing down on either side. Then, almost in the shadow of the Castle, came that maze of intersecting roadways where electric tram, motor car and horse-drawn vehicle fought a seemingly endless battle for supremacy. It always amazed me that there were not frequent collisions, for this was before the introduction of traffic signals. Somehow, however, they all managed to filter through and continue on their respective journeys.

At the time of our visits, my mother's family had spread beyond the confines of Norwich and she had just one sister living there. My father's family, on the other hand, was solidly established in the business life of the city, and this meant that we had many relatives to visit. First on the list was usually Uncle George.

Uncle George was a dealer in scrap metal and he conducted his business from a yard in St. Andrew's Street, near Charing Cross. We children all believed that he was quite well-to-do, but whenever I went into his yard I found myself thinking that, if he really was rich, why should he be content to work in such untidy surroundings? Admittedly, the yard was covered in, but everywhere one looked there was rubbish in the form of old sacks, iron piping and the like, all covered with a sturdy layer of dust. I once mentioned this problem to my mother and received the cryptic reply: "Where there's muck, there's money." This puzzled me even more for, if that really was the case, why was she herself such a stickler for cleanliness?

There was a raised platform at one end of the yard and it was there, sitting at an old wooden desk, that Uncle George carried out his dealings with prospective clients. I am not sure whether the purpose of the platform was to keep him away from the draughts which blew through the yard or whether his elevated position was designed to give him a psychological advantage as he bargained with customers. The one thing of which I am certain is that, as I craned my neck to look up at that great figure towering above me, I was filled with awe and wonderment. I soon learned, however, that there was no need for such a feeling, for he was full of kindness to me and, in fact, a truly gentle man. He was, indeed, very much in the family tradition for, whilst possessing all the attributes of an astute businessman, he was generous to a fault with people whom he liked.

I recall one visit which we paid to his yard when I was, I suppose, about eight years old. He and my mother obviously had something to discuss and, while they did so, I wandered idly round the yard gazing in wonderment at all the strange oddments piled against the walls. Then, just as their conversation was ending, a vision came into the yard in the form of a little girl, just a year or two older than me, who looked for all the world as though she had just stepped out of one of those old Victorian paintings. She wore a black, wide-skirted dress with white lace at the neck, and she had golden hair which, tied neatly with ribbon, hung loosely down her back. Her stockings were black, as also were her high lace-up boots, the top of which were hidden under her voluminous skirts.

"You mustn't go yet," said Uncle George. "Here's my little Lucy come to sing to me."

She needed very little coaxing, for she had obviously come prepared to give a performance. It had presumably happened many times before but, to me at least, it was an experience of such beauty as I had never previously encountered. She sang "Silver Threads Among the Gold" and the angelic nature of her voice was such that it would have melted the hardest heart. The sound of those golden notes echoing through that dusty old scrapyard held me entranced, but I was even more taken aback at what was to happen next. Diving his hand into his pocket, my Uncle brought out a shining half-crown which he thrust into the little girl's hand. She smiled and thanked him and then, as suddenly as she had appeared, she went skipping out of the yard.

As she disappeared up the street my Uncle turned his attention to me. "Well, Bobby, how about a song from you?" I felt my cheeks become suddenly flushed and I tried desperately to hide my face within the lapels of my coat. He was well aware that I couldn't sing, but I was not to know that he was only teasing me. "Oh well", he said, "It's only boys and girls who sing to me who get half-a-crown" and then, thrusting out his arm, he handed me a single penny. Needless to say, I was somewhat downhearted, but I accepted it with such good grace as I could muster.

My mother and I turned to leave the yard, but then, just as we neared the street, my Uncle called me back. "Let me have a look at that penny", he said. I handed it back to him and he turned it over and over in the palm of his hand. Then, closing his fist round the coin, he held it out to me. I held out my hand to catch it and he dropped it onto my palm. I looked down at the coin and my heart danced with joy. It was half-a-crown!

On leaving St. Andrew's our next destination was St. Stephen's, where my Uncles Ernest and Albert kept up the family tradition as dealers in fish and game. My mother would set off at a jaunty pace and I continually marvelled at the manner in which she was able to find her way around that vast city. I had forgotten, of course, that she had spent her early years in these surroundings and knew every little courtyard and alleyway.

I am not sure when the family's connection with fish and game began, though I have in my possession some old trade tokens of 1851 which proclaim the fact that one G. Bagshaw was at that time a dealer in such produce. My uncles, however, were destined to become the last of the line for, when drastic improvements were considered necessary in St. Stephen's, the shop was swept away and, with it, the family tradition.

I always thought that my Uncles Ernest and Albert were a somewhat unlikely pair for, at least as far as their personalities were concerned, they were as different as two men could possibly be. Albert's manner was quiet in the extreme. He was a very retiring man and his mode of speech was always respectful, frequently humble and sometimes almost apologetic. Ernest, on the other hand, was a complete extrovert. He saw the funny side of every situation and, if there wasn't a funny side, he would invent one. His impish sense of humour could be directed at anybody but, though it might sometimes be embarrassing, never was it allowed to become offensive. Above all, he had a heart of gold for, although he never allowed his astuteness in business to falter, he was ever ready to give help to anybody who needed it. Thus, deprived children were taken in convoys of cars to the seaside and, on Sunday afternoons, elderly folk were driven around the countryside. It would, in fact, have been completely impossible to count the number of lame dogs he had helped over stiles.

Acting as a kind of backroom boy at the shop was my Uncle Charles who was not a blood relative but had, in fact, married my father's sister Anna. He only rarely appeared out at the front but, instead, spent his time behind the scenes preparing the produce for sale. In my early years, in fact, I could never think of my Uncle Charles without, at the same time, visualising the great steaming vat of water in which he seemed to be perpetually boiling crabs.

To somebody of my tender years, grown-up conversation was inclined to be boring and, fond though I was of my uncles, I was always happy to be moving on, particularly as I knew that we would soon be reaching the most exciting part of our visit. Thus, my mother would lead me off into the maze of little streets and alleyways between St. Stephen's Street and St. Peter Mancroft Church and, all of a sudden, we reached the array of stalls which was the Provision Market. I have a strong feeling that the market covered a bigger area in those days, although this may be just a nostalgic quirk of my memory. Certainly, however, there was no City Hall and no War Memorial Gardens, but merely an assortment of warehouses and similar buildings extending right along St. Peter's Street and into Hay Hill. There were undoubtedly fewer stalls then than now, for they were not set out in the orderly, tightly-packed rows of today. Nor did they sparkle with the gaily-coloured candy-striped awnings which now brighten the scene. Such cover as was provided came from strips of hessian or tarpaulin or, in fact, whatever protective material the stallholders could lay their hands on. I have a strong suspicion that the conditions which prevailed were such as would bring forth cries of horror from today's Public Health authorities. Nevertheless, the whole place was a veritable wonderland, particularly for a country boy such as me.

The best time to visit the market was after dark, for then the traders would light the gas jets which illuminated the stalls, and the flickering flames would spread dancing shadows over their wares. Even more significantly, however, it was then that the traders would gradually reduce the price of their goods in an effort to clear the stall before the time came to close down for the night. Thus, for instance, oranges which, in the morning, cost a penny each (or 7 for 6d), gradually became 10 for 6d and eventually 20 for the same amount. We were particularly fond of "blood oranges", for they had thin skins and could always be relied upon to be sweet and juicy. It is many years since I saw a blood orange. I wonder why it is that so many of our childhood pleasures fail to find a place in our modern lifestyle.

Our visits to the market usually took place in the morning for it was normally part of the plan that we should have our lunch (or dinner, as we then called it) with Grandma Bagshaw, who lived in Essex Street. Thus, at the appointed time, we would make our way down to Gentleman's Walk in order to board the tram for Unthank Road. I was not yet old enough to be able to read the names on the destination boards which all the trams displayed, but I soon learned that each route had a board of a different colour. Thus it was that, as we stood on the edge of the Walk, I strained my eyes down towards the Haymarket to look for an approaching tram with a white destination board, for this was the one which would take us to the bottom of Essex Street.

If the weather was fine and we were not too heavily laden, my mother would agree to ride on the top deck, for she knew this gave me great pleasure. It was not such fun in wet weather, for the top deck, being completely open, gave no protection from the elements. One of my most amusing memories of those days is the sight of a fully laden tram ploughing its way along in a rainstorm with, on the top deck, as many as two dozen umbrellas raised in the air to shelter the passengers. It was also necessary to watch out for overhanging branches. I was too small for these to be much of a hazard but, on more than one occasion, I have seen a bowler hat whipped from a man's head and sent scuttling back along the gangway. Then there would follow a frantic dash by the owner to recapture the headgear before it bounced down the stairs to the lower deck.

The first part of our journey took place at a modest speed for, as the tram turned left into Guildhall Hill, the gradient was such that we barely achieved walking pace. On reaching St. Giles', however, the road levelled out and we began to bowl along at a steady speed which was only interrupted by the occasional stop to collect or disgorge passengers. Soon we reached Unthank Road and it was then that the driver, turning his handles with abandoned fury, let the tram have its head. The iron wheels would crash and bang and the conducting pole sent sparks flying from the overhead wires as the mighty vehicle swayed and rolled its way along. At times, on the open stretches, it would approach its maximum speed, which was said to be twelve miles an hour. I can only say that, to any traveller who experienced the joy of riding on the top deck of such a vehicle, the sensation of speed was many times greater than a mere 12 m.p.h.

All too soon our journey would be over and we would leave the tram at the bottom of Essex Street. Then it was only a hundred yards to number thirty, where my grandmother lived with her two unmarried daughters, Emma and Elsie.

I had never known my grandfather, for he had died some years before I was born. His influence was ever-present in that house, however, for his face gazed down from the parlour wall and I firmly believe that all day-to-day activities were conducted in such a manner as he would have wished. In the tradition of his family, he had been an astute businessman and had acquired investments in Government securities together with the ownership of a number of the small properties which lined those terraced streets. It was my Grandmother's task to collect the weekly rents, and she would regularly set off with her heavy black bag and cash book. Such a routine nowadays would invite the attention of the criminal fraternity, but she did it for many years without untoward incident.

Grandma Bagshaw was a jolly little woman who, although not given to bursts of outright laughter, had an almost continuous sparkle in her eyes which was ever ready to burst forth into a happy smile. She was short in stature but, in the phraseology of the day, "well-covered". Her roundness of form was, indeed, more than a little reminiscent of the dumplings which she was so fond of making. My memory tells me that she always dressed in black, but I am not sure whether this was out of continuing respect for her late husband or as a result of the strictures of her Victorian upbringing. Certainly she portrayed all that was best of the Victorian era for, although she was so full of love for her family, she held strongly to the strictest of possible beliefs concerning personal conduct. I never knew her raise her voice in anger, nor even issue a strong reprimand. She had a much subtler way of making her feelings known, particularly over such things as rudeness. For a moment her eyes would lose their sparkle and she would quietly remind the offender that "Politeness doesn't cost anything". Anybody who displayed real rudeness would be brought down to earth with "You'll catch more flies with a spoonful of sugar than a gallon of vinegar". She had one other stock phrase which, though incomprehensible when I first heard it, later served to represent to me one of her most strongly-held beliefs. This was her advice to "make spare when there's plenty", by which she meant saving for a rainy day.

There can be no doubt, however, that my most lasting memory of my grandmother was those dumplings. Just as we had Yorkshire pudding at home, so she had dumplings before coming to the meat course, and the ones she made were justly famous. I have never been madly keen on dumplings, but I have to confess that hers were something special. They were the authentic Norfolk "swimmers" which, according to tradition, must never be cut with a knife, but gently teased apart with one's fork. She would ceremoniously bring them into the dining room, piled high on an enormous dish, followed by a gigantic sauce boat filled with rich gravy. I often wonder why no dumplings since then have ever tasted quite the same. Could it be the use of different ingredients, or perhaps changed methods of cooking? Or is it, perhaps, just another case of one's memory playing tricks and investing a childhood enjoyment with an exaggerated degree of perfection?

After we had finished our meal it was frequently suggested that

I should go into the back garden and either feed the hens or water the flower beds. It was not until later in life that I realised that this was a subterfuge to get me out of the way while my elders discussed grown-up matters. Young children were kept in ignorance of much that went on in those days, particularly if it involved some sort of family crisis. I deeply regret that aspect of my boyhood, although I sometimes think that the pendulum has now swung too far in the other direction.

Anyway, the end of the discussion would lead to my being called in from the garden and then, after a cup of tea and a thick slice of Grandma's slab cake, my mother and I would start our homeward journey. I never found this as exciting as the trip we had made in the morning, partly because of the fatigue which was taking charge of my tired limbs but mostly because the element of anticipation was no longer present. Nevertheless, each of those trips to the "big city" was a high spot in my life which unfailingly gave me much to tell my schoolmates the next day.

CHAPTER 12

Tales of Mystery and Intrigue

No record of my boyhood would be complete without the mysterious tale of Miss Miles and her lavatory pan, for it was an event which held the entire population enthralled and almost brought the town to a standstill.

Every country community, large or small, had in its make-up a great diversity of characters and, with such a mixture, it was inevitable that a wealth of human characteristics should always be apparent. For the most part, life was reasonably harmonious but, at any time, there could be occasions when avarice and greed, intrigue and covetousness, or one of the many other sins of the flesh would disrupt the harmony of our little community. At a time of crisis, however, all petty jealousies and dislikes were cast aside and the people rallied together to meet it. I have never known the townsfolk to be so strongly united as they were on that fateful day when Miss Miles' lavatory pan went missing from the doorstep of her wool shop in the market place. I was a small boy at the time, but the details of the event are still vivid in my memory.

The first indication I had that a crime had been committed was when my mother and I encountered Miss Miles in the market place. She was like a woman possessed by the Devil. She was, in fact, on the verge of physical and mental collapse, for somebody had taken the lavatory pan on which she lavished such care and attention and put in its place another which was in greatly inferior condition.

Now, to understand the seriousness of the situation, it is necessary to have an appreciation of the background against which the crime was committed. North Walsham was still a backwater of rural lethargy as far as modern technology was concerned. Such of our streets as had any lighting at all were illuminated by gas lamps while the houses were lit by means of paraffin. Even more to the point, there were no flush toilets or mains drainage. Every house had its little room, usually just a wooden hut, outside at the back, where the lavatory pan was housed. Most people called it "the privy"; we called ours "the annexe".

The pan had to be emptied on a regular basis, and it was the householder's responsibility to bring it through the house and place it out on the pavement on the appointed day. Then, under cover of darkness, the "honey cart" would travel round the town to collect the contents. This cart, pulled by a single horse, carried a large metal tank into which the "honeyman" would tip his ever-increasing load. It is difficult to comprehend what kind of man could have undertaken such a task, but he was certainly providing an essential service to the community.

After the cart had gone on its way, most householders were content to give their pan a quick rinse, pop in a few drops of Lysol and replace it in the privy. This, however, was not good enough for Miss Miles. She would set to work with a will, scrubbing and polishing until her pan shone like the proverbial new pin. She had even inscribed her name upon it in bold capital letters which stood out in stark relief from the shining bodywork. It was often said, in fact, that she kept her pan in such a pristine condition that she could have eaten her breakfast porridge from it. That being so, one can well imagine her feeling of shock and horror when she opened her front door on that fateful morning and found the shabby specimen which had taken the place of her prized trophy.

The story spread through the town like wildfire. Who could have been responsible for such a dastardly deed? Who, in fact, could expect to get away with it, for Miss Miles' lavatory pan was unique. As day succeeded day, the mystery deepened and Miss Miles' suffering was painful to behold. Eventually, however, and with startling suddenness, the pan was found. It was placed on her doorstep by a nocturnal visitor, and there she found it when dawn broke over the market place. The criminal was never brought to justice, but at least the pan was back with its rightful owner.

This was not quite the end of the story for, although she was happy to have it back in her possession, she never used it again. She could not bring herself to do so because, as she herself put it, she "didn't know where it had been". Just imagine – horror of horrors – somebody else might even have sat upon it!

She bought herself a new lavatory pan on which she lavished a similar degree of loving care until, years later, she had a flush toilet installed.

There was another occasion when the townspeople became united in an effort to seek retribution for what they believed to be an injustice but, unlike the case of Miss Miles' lavatory pan, this one rapidly became coloured with sinister undertones and the threat of a violent outcome. Such a climax, in fact, was only averted by a dramatic last-minute intervention on the part of my father.

The two principal characters in this drama were the headmaster of the council school and a young orphan boy who was a classmate of mine. The orphanage stood in its own grounds on the Norwich Road and, though in all other respects a perfectly normal building, it filled us with foreboding. We had all heard tales of the rigid discipline which was enforced within its walls, and we would always cross the road in order to pass it by on the other side. The orphans themselves never seemed to be quite like the rest of us and they took little part in the activities of the other boys. Most noticeably, they rarely, if ever, smiled, but seemed instead to live their lives in a state of sombre sub-consciousness. They were never late for school and, at the end of the day, they would set off, almost like automotons, in a steady walk back to "The Home". As if that was not enough, they were always dressed in a manner which set them apart from all the other boys of the town. Whatever the weather, they unfailingly wore dark, navy blue jerseys which buttoned up on one shoulder, thick black shorts, long stockings and the heavy, black lace-up boots which were always known as "highlows".

The headmaster, as I have stated elsewhere, was a stern disciplinarian with a strong belief in the value of corporal punishment. His faith in the power of the cane was well-known throughout the town and it is probable that it was this reputation which was to bring him to the brink of disaster. In any case, there came the day when he inflicted this punishment on one of the orphan boys. There is no way of knowing how severely he treated the lad, but the story which spread around the town left nobody in any doubt that he had grossly overstepped the mark. Details of the injuries he had inflicted were spread far and wide and, influenced by the fact that the victim of the attack had nobody in the world to whom he could turn for consolation, the entire population became filled with seething anger.

On the day when this anger reached its peak, the headmaster was in Norwich, where the school choir was competing in the annual music festival. He was proud of the choir and went to great lengths to make sure that the highest possible degree of perfection was reached. Furthermore, he was very successful in this respect and, every year, the choir would bring home an assortment of banners which signified their achievements in different classes. On arrival at the railway station, the choir would line up and the head-master would then lead them through the streets to the market place, where the massed townspeople would greet them with cheering and congratulatory speeches. That was how it normally was but, on this occasion, things were to be very different.

The events of that Saturday are still vividly etched in my mind for, as the people's anger gave way to a demand for vengeance, the town became gripped in an aura of tension and fear. I well recall my parents, that afternoon, huddled together in close discussion as my father recounted the details of what the local men planned for that evening. He was as saddened as anybody about the orphan boy's punishment, but he did not approve of the manner in which things were developing. He was never a man of violence, and he feared for the outcome of the evening's happenings. He urged my mother not to go near the market place that evening and, as the fateful hour approached, he left the house.

As the minutes ticked by, my mother sat and waited in the chair by the fire. Normally she would have been knitting, or sewing, or darning, but that evening she just sat. Eventually the tension was too much, even for her. "Put on your hat and coat", she said, "We're going down to the market place".

We crept round the edge of the market place and my mother led me into the covered doorway of Mr. Jeary's sweet shop. There we huddled in the shadows and surveyed the scene. It was a vastly bigger crowd than usual and most of them were men. Furthermore, the normal excited chatter of previous years had given way to sombre muttering and the occasional call of one man's voice to another. I was very young and I suppose I was not fully capable of appreciating the seriousness of the situation. Nevertheless, I was terrified and, if it had not been for the comforting feel of my mother's hand, I would have fled the scene.

Thus we all waited for the choir to march into the market place. The minutes ticked by and, gradually, a feeling of impatience became evident. More time passed and still there was no sign of the choir. More time went by and still the crowd waited. I have no idea how long we all stood in that market place but, after what seemed an eternity, the word went round the crowd that the reception had been cancelled. The headmaster and choir had arrived at the station but had all dispersed to their various homes. Many among the crowd hung about for a time before deciding to leave, some with frustration in their hearts and others with a sense of relief. Eventually, however, the market place was empty.

Very few people ever found out the reason why North Walsham was spared a night of violence on that fateful Saturday. The answer, however, was a simple one. My father, fearing the outcome, had sent a warning message to the headmaster's wife, advising her not to venture out. A car had been sent to the station, and there the headmaster was smuggled off the train to be driven by a circuitous route to the safety of his home.

In the days which followed, the allegations against the head-master gradually became more muted until eventually they were forgotten altogether. Perhaps the townspeople felt they had punished him sufficiently by depriving him of his night of glory. Whatever the reason, it was significant that none of the orphan boys was ever again known to have been caned.

I think it is quite natural that, in our early boyhood, our lives should have been greatly coloured by the wealth of mysteries which existed in the folklore of the neighbourhood. It was an age when the idea of a man landing on the moon would have been scoffed at and instantly dismissed. Unidentified flying objects were things of the future, together with all the literary inventions of modern writers of science fiction. The mystery stories which held us enthralled were true, for they had been handed down through many generations. Some we sought out in the pages of our books, but most of them we learned from the lips of older acquaintances who, we were assured, knew the facts.

Thus, we knew all about the ghostly Anne Boleyn who, on every anniversary of her execution, revisited her childhood home at Blickling. Our minds carried a vivid picture of the white-clad spectre riding in a black, hearse-like carriage drawn by four headless horses and driven by a headless coachman. We readily visualised the scene as, with her severed head resting on her lap, she was transported up the avenue leading to the Hall. We believed it, but we had no wish to see it!

We also accepted that her father, Sir Thomas, made a yearly ride through the Norfolk countryside in a carriage drawn by headless horses, chased all the way by fiendish hounds. We had no idea of what crime he had been guilty, but we knew that the penalty he had incurred was that he must cross forty different bridges in the county on that one night.

Amongst all these mysterious figures, however, there was one which took pride of place in our imaginations and one which we would all have dearly loved to encounter. This was Old Shuck, the huge black dog which continually pads its way through a large part of the Norfolk countryside. We knew the truth about Shuck and we all wanted to help him.

Over succeeding generations, poor Shuck has become a much-maligned creature, particularly by modern writers. He has been described as a vicious character, as large as a pony, with a foaming mouth, snarling teeth and one bloodshot eye set in the middle of his forehead. His howling cry is said to strike terror into the heart of the hearer, yet his footfalls on the country lanes make no sound. Worst of all, he stands accused of pursuing the unsuspecting traveller and, with scorching breath, carrying out a vicious attack of the most appalling nature.

I very much regret the libellous nature of these descriptions of the animal, for they are completely at variance with the facts as related to me in my early boyhood. I fear that I may well be the only surviving member of the Black Shuck Appreciation Society and, as such, I feel it my duty to record the story as I first heard it.

The dog known as Shuck was, in fact, the faithful companion of a seaman who regularly navigated his small boat between the ports of Yarmouth and King's Lynn. The frequent trips, with just the man and his dog on board, took them through some of the most treacherous waters around our coastline, but somehow they always managed to battle through. One fateful night, however, strong winds whipped up the heavy seas to such an extent that the little boat could make no headway and, when the timbers began to break up under the combined force of the elements, the seaman realised that his craft was destined to go down. He could see lights in the cottage windows at Sheringham, but he knew his vessel could not make the shore.

He was resigned to losing his craft and its cargo, but it so happened that some important documents had been put into his keeping with the strict admonition that they were to be personally placed in the hands of a local dignitary at King's Lynn. These must be saved at all costs so, after rolling them inside some waterproof oilskin, he placed the bundle in Shuck's mouth and bade the dog to swim to the shore. The dog set off and, after an exhausting battle against the waves, arrived on the beach in a state of collapse. There he sat down to await the arrival of his master.

Hours passed, and still the dog waited. In the morning he was still there, his eyes searching the horizon for a sign of the seaman. Local people who had come down to the beach saw the dog and tried to take the strange package, which he still held in his mouth. The dog, however, growled in anger, for he would release it to nobody except his master. The people retreated and left the dog on the sands, still scanning the skyline and patiently waiting.

After several days had passed in this manner, the dog, probably thinking that the seaman had come ashore further along the coast, set off to search for him. As more time went by, he extended his search to a wider area, and that is why, even to this day, Black Shuck patrols that part of the Norfolk countryside. He still seeks his master and he still carries in his mouth the precious package which had been entrusted to him.

That is the story as we first heard it from an old countryman in the area. Furthermore, it endeared the dog to us and made us wish that we could find it and help to end its ceaseless search. We made frequent efforts in that respect. Sometimes, on our way home at night from a Cub meeting or similar activity, we would even make a detour through the churchyard lest the animal should be there. This, in itself, was a challenge, for the path pursued a long and winding course between the tombstones and the only illumination came from a solitary gas lamp near the halfway point.

Needless to say, we never saw Old Shuck. And, to be perfectly honest, I disbelieve any man who says he has.

CHAPTER 13

The Nook and The Terrace

Although we children were blissfully happy in our family home at "Woodland View", our stay there was destined to last for only a year or two. Then, for reasons about which we knew nothing, we found ourselves transported to the other side of the town, where we took up residence on the Norwich Road. I suspect that our move may possibly have been influenced by the cost of upkeep of our former home, for "The Nook", being a bungalow, was much smaller and, furthermore, more modern. It was, however, rather a long way from the centre of the town and this meant a lengthy walk to school. Today, I suppose, such a situation would call for the immediate provision of transport, lest we should become over-tired or get mown down by speeding traffic. The situation in those days, however, was very different, for there were few motor vehicles and, in any case, we were well accustomed to walking long distances. We went almost everywhere on foot and thought nothing of covering many miles during the course of our daily journeyings.

Throughout all the time that we lived at "The Nook" I can only recall one occasion when I had cause to regret our remoteness from the town, and even that arose solely as the result of a stroke of out-right misfortune.

Our milk came straight from the cows in those days and we had not even reached the stage where it was delivered in bottles. Instead, the milkman drove around with a massive churn, holding many gallons, on his two-wheeled cart, pulled by his sturdy and ever-patient horse. He carried with him a set of measuring cans with which he could ladle out the required amount into the customer's jug. My unfortunate experience came on an occasion when our milkman, Mr. Craske, gave me a ride on his cart. He happened to be passing the school as we came out and, as it was raining in torrents, he offered me a lift so that I could get home more quickly. I had no worry about getting wet for I was wearing my raincoat, but I accepted with alacrity, for it was not often that I had the chance of a ride on the milk cart.

All went well until we reached our house and then, as I jumped off the cart, my coat caught on the churn and toppled it over, spilling its contents onto the road. Needless to say, I was horrified. The churn could certainly not have been full, or otherwise it would not have toppled so easily. This thought did not console me, however, and, as I watched the milk mingling with the rainwater as it ran down the gutter, tears were not far away. I looked at Mr. Craske and said that I was sorry. He looked back at me and said, "Of course, your mother will have to pay for it". I fled indoors, not daring to tell my mother what had happened.

At school the next day I found it difficult to concentrate, for my mind was on other matters. At the end of the day I hurried home, fully expecting my mother to receive me with, at least, a severe reprimand. Nothing was said, however, and, as the evening wore on, my feeling of tension got the better of me.

"Has Mr. Craske been today?" I asked.

"Of course", said my mother. "He comes every day. Why should you ask such a stupid question?"

I could conceal it no longer. I blurted out my guilty secret.

The days went by and gradually I began to feel better, for nothing was ever said about the spilt milk. Dear, kind Mr. Craske had kept our little secret.

Generally speaking, however, there was an advantage to be gained from our new situation, for it meant that we were that much nearer two of our favourite hunting grounds, namely Westwick Woods and Felmingham Heath. Westwick was noted for its rhododendrons and chestnuts but, as we explored its inner recesses, we found a wealth of wildlife going about its business in the undergrowth. Bryant's Heath at Felmingham, however, was our favourite haunt and it was there that we spent many hours of boyhood bliss with picnics, games of cricket and explorations. The great thing about Bryant's Heath was that, apart from us, it was usually deserted, and it remains so today, for it is really only readily accessible on foot.

I had always had a great love of the natural world, but it was at this period of my boyhood that I began to study it in a more organised manner. My efforts in this direction were largely stimulated by my brother Arthur, who had long had a great interest in the wild flowers of the countryside and who, in fact, already had a wide knowledge of the subject. His enthusiasm soon communicated itself to me and it was he who taught me the art of pressing flowers in order to preserve them. It is a practice which I would not now recommend, for so many species have become scarce, but, at that time, there was plenty of everything.

Thus, we would lovingly gather our specimens and then, after placing them in the required position between sheets of blotting paper, we would press them between two flat pieces of wood. The actual pressing was carried out under the feet of our bed and I soon learned that it was inadvisable to press just one flower at a time. Such a practice caused the bed to stand in a very uneven position and it was somewhat difficult to sleep, with the ever-present danger of toppling out onto the floor. Consequently, I usually ensured that I had four presses going simultaneously and then, although it stood in a somewhat elevated poisition, the bed did at least remain on an even keel.

Of all the specimens with which Felmingham provided us there were two which remain strongest in my memory. These were the orchids which flourished over towards the wooded edge of the heath and, most mysterious of all, the sundews. These carnivorous beauties thrived in the marshy area and we would watch in fascination as, holding out their sticky fronds in invitation, they would lure unsuspecting insects into their trap and then close up and digest them. On a recent visit I was happy to note that the sundews still flourish on Felmingham Heath.

After a while, my parents began to feel the need for a more central position in which to live and thus it was that, in due course, we moved yet again. This time it was to be to a house which they had long coveted, for it was at the end of a row of four houses in a cul-de-sac which ran from the market place to the rear of the Paston School. It was known simply as The Terrace and ours was number four.

It was an ideal home for us all, for we had much more room to spread our wings and, though central, it was nevertheless in a secluded position. Access could only be gained on foot or, possibly, on a bicycle, and it was by no means a public thoroughfare. In spite of this, tradesmen sometimes used it as a short cut, a practice which caused my mother a certain degree of annoyance. It was a practice, furthermore, which resulted on one occasion in the quite literal downfall of our postman.

The path which ran past our house proved to be a highly suitable surface on which to make a slide in frosty weather, and Peter and I would spend long hours polishing it with our heavy boots until it presented the appearance of a miniature Cresta Run. It was in such a condition when, one wintry morning, the postman passed through on his way to the School. Then, without warning, he suddenly found himself lying flat on his back with his load of mail flying in all directions. My mother happened to witness the occurrence from our front room window and, seeing the poor man's discomfort, she could not prevent herself from bursting into a peal of laughter. Her feeling of amusement was short-lived, however, for, when the postman had eventually picked himself up and gone on his way, she noticed that he had failed to shut our gate. Cursing his thoughtlessness, she went out to remedy the situation and then, in a flash, disaster struck as she also found herself falling over backwards on our slide. I suppose it is not surprising that, from that day forward, the making of slides on our front path was prohibited.

I think Peter was the member of the family who benefitted most from our close proximity to the School for, by 1930, he had passed the Scholarship and been admitted to those hallowed halls. Thus, his daily journey to school became brief in the extreme. At the first sound of the assembly bell he would charge out of the front door, through the gate and across the yard to the school door. There he would make his entry just as the last sound from the bell rang out over the yard. He perfected his daily sprint to such a degree that never once did I know him to arrive late and thereby receive the inescapable punishment of a detention period. The fact that our windows overlooked the school was also pleasing to me, for I was able to watch the boys going about their appointed duties and I thus had a good idea of what my life would be like if, later on, I succeeded in completing our family quartet of Pastonians.

Our central situation, however, benefitted us all for, while my father was better able to keep in touch with the local community and my mother needed to spend less time in going to the shops, we also were within easy contact of the various establishments which called for our attention.

Mr. Jeary's sweet shop, naturally, was a source of great interest to us, although it must be said that it was a rather grand establishment which was mainly directed at the adult population. There was a reasonable selection of delicacies which were priced at a halfpenny or a penny and thus came within our price range. Most of us, however, suffered from permanent cash flow problems which imposed severe restrictions on our purchasing power.

Consequently, we made most of our purchases at one or other of the little sweet shops which were to be found in the back streets and alleyways of the town.

Mr. Jeary did, however, have one commodity which attracted us into his shop, and this was a fizzy drink known as Vantas. He dispensed it from a kind of inverted glass globe which stood upon his counter and, whenever we felt the need for liquid refreshment, we would pop into his shop with the request for a "ha'penny Vantas please, Mr. Jeary." Unfortunately, the drink was soon gone, and we knew that a halfpenny spent on, for instance, a mint humbug would have given a much longer-lasting pleasure. We tried to drink the Vantas as slowly as possible, but this was not easy, for Mr. Jeary was always there, hovering impatiently. He was ever eager to wash up the glass ready for the next customer.

There was really no need for us to patronise commercial establishments in order to quench our thirsts, for our mother always kept a ready supply of soft drink in her pantry. She bought lemonade crystals in a glass jar from the Star Supply Stores and regularly produced gallons of the yellow liquid which, particularly in the summer, we consumed in vast quantities. She also bought Mason's Herbal Extract, from which she produced home-brewed beer. This was quite a potent beverage which was claimed to have the additional attribute of being "good for spots". Brewing the liquid was a more lengthy process than the making of lemonade, and she would spend long hours assessing its development. Then she would painstakingly remove the scum which rose to the surface of the great earthenware bowl in which it fermented, until she considered it to be ready for bottling. It was a beverage which increased in power with keeping and sometimes, especially when my mother inadvertently used a strong mix, it developed a frightening degree of potency. There were many occasions when in the depths of night the whole household would be awakened by the sound of one of the bottles exploding in the cellar.

Just around the corner from the market place was the barber's shop where Mr. Newson provided haircuts at a charge of 4d for men and 2d for boys. I have never enjoyed having my hair cut for, though I have no dislike of the actual process, I have always regarded it as a waste of valuable time. Even as a child I would always be thinking of what I could have been doing if I was not restricted by the confines of Mr. Newson's chair. I suppose it was the lack of concentration which caused me to be a somewhat restless subject. Whatever it was, Mr. Newson was never very happy with the situation, and he was constantly haranguing me and telling me to keep my head still.

I tried very hard, but we eventually reached the stage when he issued his final threat. "If you don't keep your head still", he said, "you will have to pay the grown-up's rate". This finally did the trick, for under no circumstances could I tell my mother that my next haircut would cost fourpence. I therefore concentrated every nerve and sinew in an effort to remain immobile. I gripped the arms of the chair until my knuckles turned a ghostly white. I put every ounce of power I possessed into a supreme effort to make sure that Mr. Newson would not carry out his threat. Happily, I succeeded, but my visits to the hairdresser thereafter were always fraught with tension lest I should incur his wrath.

One of the regular duties which we boys had to undertake was the weekly visit to Mr. Fayers' bakehouse, which was tucked away in one of the little lokes which ran off the market place. With the ever-present need to satisfy the appetites of four growing lads, my mother did much baking and every week, apart from the smaller items, she would prepare four large fruit cakes, each weighing several pounds. These she did not bake herself, however, for, in common with a number of other housewives, she had an arrangement with Mr. Fayers whereby he carried out the process for her. Thus, when he had finished producing his bread, he would put the cakes in his still-warm oven and bake them through for a charge of one penny per cake. So it was that one of us was required to take the cakes to the bakehouse on our way to school and to collect them when we came home.

This was an arrangement which worked extremely well for all concerned for, while Mr. Fayers made a profit from heat which would otherwise have been wasted, my mother was able to ensure that, for just a few coppers, she always had a ready supply of fruit cake on her pantry shelves. Furthermore, the quality of the finished product was something out of this world. I can honestly say that never since my childhood days have I eaten fruit cake which gave me such pleasure and satisfaction.

In all the many weekly visits which we made to the bakehouse, I can only remember one occasion when the system broke down. My brother Arthur had been the errand boy on this occasion and, when he brought home the four cakes, my mother inspected them with her usual close scrutiny. Then, flinging up her hands in horror, she declared that one of them was not hers. Certainly, the cake in question was a rather pathetic specimen, being dry and shrivelled and somewhat black in colour. We will never know whether it was, in fact, somebody else's cake or whether it had been put too far into the oven and was merely over-baked. Whatever the truth of the matter might have been, my mother would not accept it and Arthur was duly despatched to return it to the bakehouse. Mr. Fayers was at a loss for an explanation, but he did not want to upset such a good customer.

"Leave it with me", he said, "and I'll see what I can do".

Sure enough, the matter was rectified for, the next day, my mother received a freshly-baked fruit cake of the very highest quality. Presumably Mr. Fayers had made it specially for her. Anyway, my mother was pacified and, from then on, the system continued to work with never a semblance of a hitch.

Thus, our life at The Terrace pursued its steady course, with barely a ripple to disturb the smoothness of our existence. One day followed another with a degree of sameness which ought to have been monotonous but which never was. We were living our lives in the manner which was expected of us. We were conforming to a long-established pattern which, even then, showed little sign of any of the changes which were lying hidden in the years ahead.

Above all, I suppose, we were conforming to tradition and this is nowhere more noticeable than in our attitude to the various high days and holidays which had their place in the country calendar. The farm worker still took his plough to be blessed in the church on Plough Monday and watched the weather conditions on Candlemas Day to see whether winter had really gone or whether it would have "another flight". Pancakes were an essential part of Shrove Tuesday, just as Good Friday would not have been right and proper without real hot cross buns. May Day really was the first day of May and not the political Bank Holiday which it has now become. The maypole, dragged out of its hiding place and decorated with garlands, was the focus of the children's dancing on that most festive of days.

Even Oakapple Day had its place in our calendar, and few people failed to wear a buttonhole of oak leaves on May 29th. We were not really aware that we were celebrating Charles II's escape from Cromwell's troops back in 1651, but we knew that tradition demanded that we should wear a sprig of oak on that day. The girls, indeed, knew that failure to conform to this practice meant that the boys had the right to whip their legs with stinging nettles. I have never been able to discover any historical significance in this part of the day's activities. I suppose one must just regard it as an early example of male chauvinism.

Of all the year's festivals, however, there can be no doubt that it was Christmas which brought the greatest feeling of joy into our lives. I am convinced that there was much more true happiness in those old Christmasses than there is today, for our expectations were simple and, furthermore, there was not the unduly long build-up which has now become an accepted part of the festive season. With the exception of such things as the cakes and puddings, most of the preparations were left almost until the last minute and it was not until Christmas Eve that most of the essential shopping was done. Then the butchers' shops would be packed with great carcasses of beef and mutton, and long strings of unplucked fowls and unskinned rabbits would hang out on display. There, too, would be the great piles of Christmas trees from which we would select the one which would grace our front sitting room.

It was always the tradition that the tree was not decorated until very late on Christmas Eve. It would be positioned in the corner of the room, and there it would stand in all its wild nakedness until we younger children were safely installed in our beds. We knew that it was Father Christmas, in fact, who would decorate it when he called to leave our presents. Then, when we came down the stairs the next morning, that bare tree would have been transformed into a scintillating wonderland of colour and light. I would strongly recommend this practice to present-day parents of young children, for the feeling of joy and wonderment with which that sight flooded my young mind is something which has stayed in my memory ever since. It was the one thing above all others which convinced me that Christmas Day was, indeed, the most special day of the whole year.

It has been said by a contemporary that a "fiver" was sufficient in those days to buy each member of the family a present and still leave enough for the fruit and nuts and the festive drinks. There is, no doubt, much truth in that statement, but it tends to give a false impression for, although most people found it necessary to keep their spending on a tight rein, we never felt that we were in any way deprived of the good things of life. With the help of presents from our aunts and uncles in Norwich, our Christmas stockings were always full of a multitude of mysteries. Most of the toys and games were simple things such as ludo, halma and tiddleywinks but these, together with a selection of books and an assortment of fruit and nuts, ensured that the empty pillowcases which hung from our beds on Christmas Eve were full to overflowing when we awoke the next morning.

So it was that all the excitement of Christmas was packed into just a few short days, with even the Christmas cards being delivered on Christmas morning rather than weeks before. I suppose it could be said that our celebration of Christmas was a reflection of the simple, uncluttered nature of our lives in those days. Simple it may have been, but it was full of a spirit of joy and contentment which now exists only in one's memory.

CHAPTER 14
The 12-plus Boy

The dawning of each successive New Year was never greeted with any great degree of enthusiasm, for there were no bank holidays to celebrate the occasion and, for most families, the chances of its being any different from the year which had preceded it were remote in the extreme. Thus it was with the arrival of 1931 for, although I knew only too well that this was the year when I was to sit for the Scholarship, it seemed otherwise to be just like most of the others. In the event, however, it was to be a fateful year in the lives of our entire family, and one which was to have a particularly marked effect on my peaceful progress through life.

I was not unduly concerned about my approaching examination, for I found little difficulty in any of my schoolwork. I have no wish to give the impression that I was a horrible little swot, for nothing was further from the truth. It was just that I found a constant fascination in words and figures, and I loved using them in every possible way. Even so, I gradually became aware of the fact that I was now expected to concentrate even more strongly on my preparation for the examination.

I cannot remember any great degree of emphasis being placed upon this in school, for there it seemed that things went along in much the same way as usual. I suppose this was understandable, for it must be admitted that many of my young contemporaries had no academic leanings, and a grammar school career had little to offer them. At home, however, I detected a slight quickening of the family pulse and I soon became aware of the importance of doing well.

The urgings I received from my parents and elder brothers came not so much from direct statements but rather by means of slightly subtle hints. In various parts of the house where I was known to occasionally settle I would find sheets of notepaper and well-sharpened pencils to occupy my odd moments. In other strategic positions there would be the occasional text book casually lying open at a page which contained some fact or problem which was considered worth memorising. The only really direct tactic which I recall was the time when I was taken to Yarmouth and given a full day's study of the activities of the herring fishing fleet. There I learned such things as the difference between a trawler and a drifter as I watched the "silver darlings" being landed and then being gutted by the Scottish "fisher lassies". It was known that I would have to write an essay in my exam, and it was thought that this might provide a suitable subject.

So, as the early weeks of 1931 pursued their inexorable course, I applied myself to the task of absorbing everything which was available in order that I could achieve the success which was expected of me.

It was then that Fate took a hand in my life and dropped a veil of uncertainty over my future. It began with my father's transfer to the head office of the "Eastern Daily Press" in Norwich, a fact which meant, of course, that we must leave North Walsham. This in itself did not appear to pose any problems until it was realised that we would be moving before the date of my exam. Even this gave me no cause for concern, however, for could I not take it in Norwich? Unfortunately, the answer to this question was "No", for it transpired that the City Education Authority used a different qualification date and the exam in Norwich was to take place before we took up residence there. It was at this point that I had my first practical experience of the wondrous workings of officialdom.

In view of my unfortunate position, could I be allowed to come to Norwich and take the exam before we actually left North Walsham? "No", said officialdom. I would at that stage still be classed as a "County boy" and, as such, could not take a City exam.

Well, then, could I be allowed to return to North Walsham and take the exam after we had moved to Norwich? "Oh, No", said officialdom. I would by then have become a "City boy" and, as such, could not take a County exam.

The only concession that could be made was that I would be allowed to take the exam in Norwich the following year. Even then, I would be required to achieve a higher standard, for I would then be officially classified as a "12-plus boy".

There was no alternative but to accept the situation, and I thus faced the prospect of a further year of council school education. This was at first a source of great disappointment to me but, in the event, that period was to become one of great significance in my life and one which I am now glad not to have missed.

We duly took our leave of North Walsham and arrived at our new home in the Lakenham area of the city. There, the various members of our family applied themselves to the task of adapting to a new way of life. While my mother busied herself with her domestic duties, my father took up his new position in the London Street office where he was later to become Chief Reporter. Arthur, meanwhile, had decided to enter the dental profession and, to this end, was now studying at the London Hospital. Stanley, in the footsteps of his father, had chosen journalism and was attached to the Yarmouth office of the paper. I suppose Peter was the one mostly affected by our move, for he now faced the daily journey to North Walsham to continue his schooling at Paston. There had been much pressure from official quarters to bring about his transfer to the City of Norwich School, but my mother strongly resisted this. Peter, for his part, accepted his daily 30-mile journey with equanimity.

My own schooling entered into its new phase with my admission to Lakenham Council School, just a few hundred yards along the road from our home. I must confess that I arrived there with certain misgivings, for I had a strong fear that a school full of city children would be a somewhat sterner setting than the happy establishment which I had just left. I soon realised, however, that I need not have harboured such a fear, for I immediately settled into my new surroundings and proceeded to enjoy a period of unalloyed happiness.

There were, of course, some basic differences from North Walsham, the most notable being that I was once again back in a mixed school of boys and girls and, furthermore, that my education was once more in the hands of a woman teacher. The classes, indeed, were even larger than those to which I had been accustomed but, in spite of the fact that we, in Class 4, numbered 49, Mrs. Dix succeeded with apparent ease in communicating with each and every one of us.

In my own case, her success in that respect is borne out by the fact that, at the end of that first term, I came top of the class. I well remember my mother's smile of pleasure when she heard this news, for she must earlier have wondered how I would settle into my changed situation. So, as that Summer term of 1931 came to an end, there was pleasure all round and my little world was full of happiness.

Suddenly, however, all this was to change when, without warning, the Education Authority decided to bring to an end their earlier policy of co-education in schools. Lakenham, it was decreed, was to become an all-girls establishment, and the boys were to be packed off to St. Mark's School in Hall Road. Thus came another dramatic change in my life and, with it, a resurgence of the doubts which I had earlier harboured when I came under the wing of Mrs. Dix. Once again, however, these doubts were to be short-lived for, whilst Lakenham had given me happiness, my year at St. Mark's was destined to be one of sheer bliss.

To begin with, we were, of course, all boys and we considered this to be a great improvement. Furthermore, we were now divided into Forms instead of Classes and, what is more, we were henceforth to be known as Scholars instead of Pupils. Being officially designated as Senior Scholars in Form 1a did wonders for our confidence. We really did begin to think that, at last, we were people of some importance.

There was one other fact about St. Mark's which was destined to have a great bearing on my personal future, and this was that the headmaster, Mr. Snell, was an Old Pastonian. He endeavoured, as far as possible, to run his school on the same lines as Paston and, when he heard of my mother's wish that I should be the fourth of her sons to go to his old school, he vowed to do everything in his power to help me. Both he and my form master, Mr. Read, were as good as their word and it seemed that, in whatever activity I might be engaged, I was to find support and encouragement on all sides.

It is certainly true that, at least until the age of twelve, my schooldays were the happiest of times. In qualification of this, furthermore, it must be said that my year at St. Mark's transcended all that had gone before. Even so, the pleasures of life did not all stem from school, for the very fact that we now lived in the city meant that there was always a wealth of attractions to be sought out and savoured.

One of the greatest of these was Lakenham Cricket Ground, which was almost on our doorstep and was the setting for the matches played by Norfolk County Cricket team. I always had a great interest in nearly every kind of sport, and the nearness of this mecca was too great an attraction to be ignored. I suppose the standard of play was probably nothing when compared with that which the likes of Jack Hobbs and Herbert Sutcliffe were exhibiting in first-class cricket at that time. Nevertheless, the sporting prowess of such as Michael Falcon, the Rought-Rought brothers and G.N. Scott-Chad drew me like a magnet. Long before the first ball was bowled I would arrive with my packet of sandwiches and a bottle of lemonade, and there I would stay until the close of play. I watched every ball and applauded every scoring stroke, and then, on the next day, I would be back to see it all over again. And, of course, the strange thing is that the sun always shone. At least, that is what my memory tells me!

In the winter it was, of course, football which occupied my thoughts and, though I much preferred playing the game rather than watching, I did make occasional forays up the hill to "The Nest" to watch the Canaries do battle. As with so many other traditional features of the city, Norwich City Football Club presents a somewhat different spectacle in these days of high-powered business acumen and sponsorship. Nevertheless, there was always something a little bit special about watching the likes of Varco and "Ginger" Smith displaying their skills in that quaint little hillside arena.

Above all, however, it was the City itself which claimed my attention and I spent long hours on journeys of exploration through its winding streets. It was not so much the Cathedral, the Castle and the other fine buildings which attracted me, magnificent though they were. It was rather more the narrow little thoroughfares and alleyways which drew me under their spell, together with the multitude of old yards which sheltered behind them. These, in truth, were in many cases little more than slums where sometimes as many as six or seven families lived in poverty with no indoor sanitation or running water. Thankfully, conditions are very different nowadays, but I will always retain the memory of those exciting trips of discovery through the back streets of the city. I continually extended my range and, in the course of time, I steadily built up a knowledge of the thoroughfares of Norwich which would surely have been the envy of many a taxi driver or delivery man.

Furthermore, it was not only the streets themselves which drew my interest, but also the wealth of little shops, particularly those devoted to the sale of secondhand books. Row upon row of old volumes were displayed on shelves outside the shops and, though I was rarely sufficiently affluent to make a purchase, I studied them all with the greatest enthusiasm. There was one happy occasion when, for the sum of one penny, I bought an old copy of Davenport's "Introduction To Zoology". It was not only the subject matter which appealed to me, but also the fact that it had previously been in the ownership of a man of some repute. Within the front cover, indeed, was a plate bearing a family crest and the statement that, in 1900, it had been in the library of one Robert Gurney. The book still occupies a proud place on my shelves.

Most of my exploration was done on foot but, particularly when I was going further afield, I frequently went on my bicycle. Riding such a machine through the city streets involved very little danger, for there was considerably less traffic in those days and what there was moved in a much more leisurely fashion than that of today. The only real hazard was the tramway system. I have often regretted that Norwich got rid of its trams, but I have to admit that they did sometimes pose problems for the cyclist. To be correct, it was not so much the trams themselves as the rails on which they ran, for they were just the right width to accommodate a cycle wheel and, once caught, it was not easy to get it free without dismounting. Failure to do this usually meant that rider and machine would part company in a most violent manner, and this happened to me on a number of occasions.

The most frequent scene of this catastrophe was at the end of Rampant Horse Street where I turned to the left to make my way to Castle Meadow. I must confess that I was in the habit of travelling at a fair speed but this presented no problem while I was able to

An old Norwich tram passes Barn Road on its journey
from the Royal Hotel to Dereham Road.

maintain full control of my machine. If my front wheel became caught in the tram line, however, the inevitable happened and, while my bicycle flew across the road in the direction of Westlegate, my body went bumping along the cobbles towards Orford Place. I always promised myself that I would be more careful next time, but, somehow, I never learned my lesson.

The effect of getting caught in the tramlines was even more dramatic for some of the early motor cars, particularly the Trojan with its narrow wheels and solid rubber tyres. The wheel and the tramline were apparently a perfect fit and there was no escape. The only solution was for the motorist to follow the lines all the way to the terminus, where he could regain the safety of the open road. I often wondered what would happen if he met an oncoming tram on the way but, somehow or other, the problem was always resolved.

CHAPTER 15

Yesterday's Norwich

To say that Norwich has changed much in the past fifty years would be to state the obvious. To chronicle the transformation which has taken place in the city would, indeed, fill many volumes, for anybody who has lived through that period has probably been witness to a more dramatic succession of developments than at any other time in history. Furthermore, the change does not stem merely from buildings and thoroughfares, but, even more, from the totally changed mode of life which has developed in that short period of time.

Slums have been swept away and replaced by large housing estates on all the city's fringes. Horse-drawn traffic has given way to the ever-increasing cannibalism of the motor vehicle. Outside toilets and oil lamps are things of the past, together with the kitchen copper and the black-leaded cooking range. The old silent films have become museum pieces in the face of the sophisticated colour spectacles which daily fill the screens in cinemas and on television sets. The summer holiday at Hemsby has given way to a fortnight on the Costa-del-Somewhere or, perhaps, a flight on Concorde.

Amidst all these changes, however, there is one which, to a countryman, stands out almost above all others, and this is the way in which the city appears to have gradually severed any direct connection with its agricultural environs. In the thirties the countryside was on the city's very doorstep, but successive developments for housing and industry have pushed it steadily back into an ever-shrinking county. Then, of course, the city's agricultural heart was torn out with the transfer of the Cattle Market to Harford Bridges in 1960.

For many generations that vast slope in the shadow of the Castle had, every Saturday, been the temporary resting place for countless sheep and cattle, horses and pigs, poultry and game, all adding their own particular aroma to the heady scent which wafted over the area. Indeed, it was not merely an aroma which they provided for, as one walked along Farmer's Avenue and turned down Cattle Market

In the days when the Cattle Market nestled in the shadow of the Castle, Norwich acquired a distinctly agricultural aroma.

Street, rubber boots became very much the order of the day. I suppose it is much more convenient to have a nice big car park in the centre of the city, but somehow it never seems the same without the regular weekly squealing and grunting, lowing and cackling of its erstwhile visitors.

It was, indeed, not only the Cattle Market itself which took on a rural look on those past Saturdays, for the effects of such an agricultural presence spread far and wide throughout the city. Most of the cattle were driven through the streets on their way both to and from the market and the whole day tended to consist of a series of confrontations between startled beasts and even more startled shoppers, all mingling with the medley of trams, carts and early motor cars which filled the thoroughfares. Frequently a sheep or cow would detach itself from its colleagues and decide to take a stroll through the open doorway of a shop, much to the consternation of the people within. And yet, in spite of the confusion which it inevitably brought with it, the Cattle Market was never resented, for it was, indeed, an integral part of the city. It really and truly belonged. Now, of course, all that has gone and, with it, the Agricultural Hall.

It is not strictly true to say that the Agricultural Hall has gone, for it still stands and forms part of the Anglia Television complex. In its heyday, however, it was one of the finest buildings in Norwich and played host to a variety of activities. As its name implies, its main purpose was to provide the setting for livestock shows and similar events, but this was by no means its only use. When the two big fairs arrived each year at Easter and Christmas, every inch of the Cattle Market was filled, right up to the edge of the Castle Mound. Then, to enable the visitors to enjoy the various delights of the fair even in bad weather, many more rides, together with hoop-la stalls and the like, were housed within the hall's protective covering.

The Agricultural Hall also played host to a variety of trade exhibitions and similar functions, none of which was more memorable than the Ideal Homes Exhibition. This was something quite unique for Norwich, for it housed everything from the smallest item of kitchen equipment to an entire bungalow. By far the greatest of its attractions, however, was the huge illuminated fountain which, to the music of a string orchestra, threw cascades of water over a large area in the middle of the Hall.

Another building which served to maintain the connection between Norwich and its agricultural roots was the Corn Exchange, known to everybody more simply as the Corn Hall. This building, standing at the corner of Exchange Street and Bedford Street, was both a business centre and a social rendezvous for the farming fraternity. Like the Agricultural Hall, it also had its other uses, notably as a centre for auction sales where literally anything could be bought and sold. It also served as a place of entertainment, particularly for followers of the sport of boxing, and it was here that such local heroes as Ginger Sadd, Snowy Edwards and Jack Forster displayed their skills. As with the Cattle Market and the Agricultural Hall, the Corn Exchange was destined to outlive its usefulness and eventually it was demolished to make room for a commercial building.

Thus Norwich severed its three strongest links with the world of agriculture on which so much of its earlier prosperity had been founded. I suppose it is true that, in the modern-day world, nostalgia doesn't pay the rent. Nevertheless, I am rather glad that, in my boyhood years, the city was only half industrial and half pastoral.

Life proceeded at a steady pace and with an overall impression of unhurried calm which, incidentally, was reflected in many of the

Sunday afternoon band concerts in Eaton Park attracted large audiences –
and nearly everybody wore a hat!

spare-time pursuits in which the people of the city engaged. Sunday afternoon band concerts at Eaton Park and Chapelfield Gardens attracted large audiences. For others there was the tram ride to the terminus at the Redan, followed by a stroll to Thorpe Gardens and a quiet hour by the riverside. The more energetic types took themselves down to the boathouse at Heigham, where they hired a rowing boat or a canoe for a trip up the Back River to Hellesdon Mill. At the band concerts formality was the order of the day but, on the river, the reverse was the case. Even so, a certain degree of navigational skill was called for in order to avoid incurring the wrath of the occasional angler and, in particular, the frolicking bathers at the Eagle swimming bath. The Eagle, incidentally, was not really a swimming bath, but merely a stretch of the river set aside for bathers and equipped with diving boards and wooden bathing huts. It was all very modest and unassuming, but the Back River on a sunny summer's afternoon was a haven of delight for the undemanding pleasure-seekers of that era.

Overshadowing all the simple pastimes of the thirties, however, there was a more sophisticated form of entertainment which was gradually becoming firmly established, for this was the beginning of the heyday of the cinema. Norwich, indeed, became extremely well-served in this respect. There must have been at least a dozen cinemas, each with a complete change of programme at least once every week, and Peter and I must in due course have patronised them all. Even so, we had our favourites and there were just a few where we became regular visitors.

Two of these, the Regent and the Electric, stood almost cheek by jowl on Prince of Wales Road. The Regent was the grander of the two, with artistic murals and, on the first landing, an ornamental pool with huge goldfish and perpetually-playing fountains. The Electric was very much the poor relation, with older films and lower admission charges. The management later changed its name to the Norvic and adopted the practice of supplying their afternoon patrons with a free cup of tea. The Regent retaliated by introducing live variety acts in addition to the usual programme of films. The Norvic was later demolished, but the Regent still survives, though in the modern guise of a multi-screen cinema.

My favourite cinema, however, was the Haymarket, which nestled along the edge of Hay Hill on a site now occupied by a department store. It was quite a grand place, with frescoes on the walls and ceilings and an overall atmosphere of opulence. It also had the added attraction of its "mighty Compton organ", on which a musician named John Bee played popular music in the intervals. The organ would rise up out of the floor at the end of the first half, and the dapper little organist would already be at the console, playing away merrily as his instrument carried him into view. John Bee was very popular and, furthermore, he was destined to become the means by which I was regularly to gain free access to the cinema. It all arose from a lesson at school.

A few yards away from the cinema stood St. Peter Mancroft Church and, in between, there was a statue of Sir Thomas Browne, sitting in his chair with his head resting on his hand. I did not, at that time, realise that Sir Thomas had achieved fame as a philosopher and physician and that, furthermore, he had lived in 17th century Norwich.

On the day in question, our form master was relating the achievements of many renowned citizens of Norwich in earlier times. When he asked us to name some of our famous ancestors, we did our best with such as Nurse Cavell, Amelia Opie and so on. Then we could think of no more. "I'm surprised at you", said Mr. Read. "There is one man you should all know about, for he is always there whenever you pass the Haymarket. There he sits, hour after hour, never getting tired . . ." At this point, I knew the answer. My hand shot up and I found myself blurting out, "Please, sir! John Bee, sir!" My colleagues murmured in agreement. Mr. Read, however, just stood there and smiled. He had, of course, meant Sir Thomas Browne.

My moment of embarrassment, however, later had a happy sequel for, somehow or other, the story reached the ears of John Bee himself. He was apparently flattered to know of the existence of his young fan and he sent me a message of thanks, together with the promise that, whenever I wanted to visit the Haymarket Cinema, I had merely to ask for him and I would be admitted free of charge. Thus, for many months, I was able to see all the latest films in cost-free comfort.

In spite of the ready availability of organised entertainment, we still made most of our own amusement. The majority of Peter's friends were, of course, at school in North Walsham, but I had many in our area, including the son and daughter of our next-door neighbours. We shared many childhood pursuits and, at one time, developed a precocious belief in our ability as theatrical entertainers. We produced a number of little shows, which we presented under the pompous title of "The City Road Juveniles". I feel sure our respective parents were duly impressed although I have no recollection of our fame spreading far beyond our own domain.

Moving to Norwich had also brought us into closer contact with the many branches of the family which were spread around the city. At one time we left Lakenham and, for a brief period, lived in a little house in Essex Street. I never knew the reason for this move, but I later deduced that it was in order that we might be nearer my grandmother, who was then suffering from a terminal illness. The move brought us more into the heart of things and it was then that we began to spend much time in the company of our cousins, Ernest and Alan Driver, who lived in Glebe Road. We formed ourselves into a Club which, by means of a cunning juxtaposition of part of our respective surnames, we called "The Dribags". We then challenged other similar groups of boys to contests at such worldly pursuits as darts, rings, bagatelle and whist. Even at this stage in our youth (Peter and Ernest were both fourteen) the lure of the cigarette card was still very strong, and it was customary for both clubs to put down 50 cards as stake money, with the winners scooping the pool. The highlight of the season was always our match against the "Three Feathers Club", which consisted of Sidney Leman and the two Heckford brothers.

It was the accumulation of material wealth in the form of cigarette cards which also led us to organise fetes and garden parties in our respective gardens. The only surviving copy of "The Dribags Club Magazine" (which was, in fact, the only one which was ever produced) reports that such a function was held on August 6th 1932 in "the spacious grounds of Glebe Court" (actually No. 92 Glebe Road) "by kind permission of Lady Driver" (our Aunt Anna). The total proceeds amounted to 650 cards, which were later shared on a sliding scale according to the degree to which it was considered we had individually contributed to the success of the afternoon. I note that Peter and Ernest each received 240 cards whilst my share amounted to 120. Young Alan's help was apparently not highly regarded, for he received just 40.

After the death of my grandmother, we moved house yet again. This time it was to another family-sized house on the other side of the city in the village of Thorpe St. Andrew. It was to be my final boyhood home.

Contact with other branches of the family remained strong and, although at first we had no car, travelling presented little difficulty. My Uncle Ernest would call on us and take my mother and me for a trip into the country or an afternoon at Yarmouth. Then there were the visits to my Uncle George's seaside home at Caister.

I recall one such trip when, on arrival, we found the house completely full of uncles and aunts. I think every one of them must have been there, but I was immediately despatched into the garden with instructions to water the flower beds. After what seemed an eternity, I was called back into the house for tea and fruit cake, together with my reward of half-a-crown. This was to be repeated on more than one occasion and, although I was told nothing at the time, I later deduced that it was some kind of family conference at which my young presence was not considered desirable.

Family cooperation was notable in many facets of life, even extending to the purchase of coal. Thus, it was the regular practice of one of my uncles to obtain this fuel in bulk, ordering it by the railway wagonload direct from the Welsh pit where it was mined. The wagon would then make the rail journey across the country to the old Midland station in Norwich, where it was transferred to lorries for delivery to the various family homes. I doubt whether the local coal merchants looked kindly upon this practice, but I gather it was quite an economical method of purchasing the winter fuel.

All this time, my twelfth birthday came steadily nearer and, with it, the prospect of sitting for the Scholarship. My mother continued in her determination that I should go to Paston, and I knew only too well what was expected of me. Even so, I was not unduly bothered, for I was happy at St. Mark's and found no great difficulty in satisfying the demands of the masters. When the fateful day arrived, I cannot remember it as being much different from any other end-of-term exam. Anyway, I did what was required to the best of my ability and we then awaited the outcome.

I have no recollection of the length of that waiting period but, when the results were announced, they were received with great joy for I had, indeed, passed. I had won that coveted place at grammar school.

It was then, however, that officialdom once again reared its ugly head, and it appeared that my mother's great ambition was to be thwarted at the last hurdle. I had, indeed, achieved the standard required of a "12-plus boy", but the fact that I had done it in a City exam meant that I could only go to a Norwich grammar school. I was awarded a place at the City of Norwich School and under no circumstances could I be given a place at Paston. This was something which my mother was not prepared to accept and she immediately declared a state of war between herself and the education authorities.

The Norwich authority stood firm and declared that it was to be the City of Norwich School or nothing. A personal plea to the headmaster of C.N.S. fared no better and merely brought advice on the clothing I would be required to wear and the manner in which I would be expected to behave at his school. At that point, my mother made her last big effort in the form of an appeal to Major Pickford, the headmaster at Paston. The result was, more or less, the same, for he had no power to alter the existing rules. He offered a glimmer of hope, however, by referring the matter to the Board of Governors at Paston.

They, in their turn, considered my position with a high degree of understanding and finally announced that they were prepared to offer me a place at Paston, but it would involve the payment of what was called the "non-Norfolk fee" of £21 per annum. In today's affluent society, that small sum may well appear to be trivial in the extreme. At the time, however, it represented a rather large slice of my parents' available income. Furthermore, they also faced the cost of school uniform and sports clothing, together with the expense of my six-days-a-week rail journey to North Walsham.

Major Pickford described the imposition of the fee as "a scandalous thing", but he nevertheless offered another tenuous lifeline. "Your boy", he wrote, "must come along and beat all the other boys in the form and I shall then have a good case at the end of the year for recommending him for that rare award – a Paston Scholarship, which would entitle him to free tuition".

This was enough for my mother. I would go to Paston and, furthermore, I would then win the Paston Scholarship. There was no doubt about it – her mind was made up. At no time in those lengthy negotiations, of course, was I consulted concerning my views on the matter. To be honest, it would not have changed things in the slightest, for I dearly wanted to go to Paston and I was quite prepared to take up the challenge. There were times when I believed it to be somewhat unfair that I was required, in effect, to pass two scholarships in order to go to one school. Nevertheless, if that was the way it had to be, I was prepared to accept it and to endeavour to do what was expected of me. Thus, the decision was made. My City Scholarship was declined and preparations were made for my entry into Paston.

Fortunately for me, there was a slight breathing space before this transition was to take place, for it was July and there was a whole summer holiday to be enjoyed first. I thus pushed all thoughts of schooling to the back of my mind and set about the business of enjoying the weeks which lay ahead. The sun shone, and life was sweet. I savoured every minute of that last period of freedom. I am so thankful I did, for my life was never quite the same again.

CHAPTER 16

In Nelson's Footsteps

In the year 1769, having received some early tuition at the Royal Grammar School in Norwich, eleven-year-old Horatio Nelson moved on to Sir William Paston's School at North Walsham. There, in company with his older brother William, he was to receive his main education at the hands of an elderly French teacher and a headmaster "of the flogging tradition". In this rather small establishment Nelson minor studied until, in 1771 and still many months away from his thirteenth birthday, he became a midshipman on the 64-gun ship Raisonnable under the command of his uncle, Captain Maurice Suckling.

In the year 1932, having received more than a little education at a variety of establishments, Bagshaw minor moved on to the Paston School, where his older brother Peter had already been in attendance for two years. There, for the next four years, he was to encounter such a diversity of experiences as would leave him well-prepared for anything which life could throw at him in later years. Happiness and depression, success and failure – all were there in full measure, delicately woven into the intricate tapestry of life which was the inescapable penalty of becoming a "grammar school boy".

Paston had changed much since Nelson had walked within its walls, but his influence could still be felt and was to surface again in tangible form later in my life. On arrival I found myself suddenly plunged into a fraternity numbering something over 200 – small by today's standards, but frighteningly large when compared with the intimate groups in which I had previously received my tuition.

The old School House and library, originally so isolated, had been joined at different periods by a diversity of other buildings which, with the addition of a high brick wall, surrounded a large, asphalt-covered open space. This, of course, was the equivalent of the playground at our more junior establishments. We soon learned, however, that to refer to it as such was to invite ridicule and accusations of "baby talk". It was known simply as "The Yard". Little playing actually took place in the Yard and, at a certain point in every day's routine, it was, in fact, the scene of an activity which we considered far removed from play. On the ringing of the mid-morning bell, we were required to emerge from our various formrooms, strip to the waist, and engage in twenty minutes of organised physical jerks under the command of the gym master and supervised by the other members of the staff. This took place every day irrespective of prevailing weather conditions. Even in extremes of frost and snow the entire school emerged into the open to engage in this barbaric practice – they in their overcoats and scarves and we in our half-naked defencelessness. We were told by the gym master that the purpose of the exercise was to "blow all the froust off of you!" We would have much preferred to have left the froust undisturbed.

I must return briefly to the Nelson influence, for it was to be with me throughout my remaining schooldays and into adult life. Paston was proud of its most illustrious son, and part of the library was given up to a display of Nelson memorabilia. There was his pencil box and also the desk where he had "taken up his station against the wall, between the parlour door and the chimney; the latter to the right". Also there, in its own little glass case, was the wall brick bearing the initials 'H.N.' – allegedly carved by the future hero's own hand. This last exhibit was a source of inspiration to many of us, and I would strongly recommend a tour of inspection of the wall surrounding the Yard. There the interested observer will find several dozen bricks all bearing the magic initials "H.N." Ignoring the fact that the wall was of comparatively recent erection, we all brought our artistic talents into play in the mistaken belief that the bricks might become collectors' items.

The school was divided into four "houses", each named after an illustrious former pupil. Admiral Sir William Hoste and Archbishop Tenison were recognised by two of the houses, whilst a third bore the name of a man named Wharton. The reason for his fame eludes my memory, though I believe he is remembered as a theologian and preacher. The fourth, of course, had to be Nelson, and it was into this house that I was admitted and in which I was expected to continue the exploits and achievements of my brothers. Soon I would be proudly wearing the yellow and black chequered shirt of Nelson House and carrying it to glory in a wealth of sporting events, just as did my earlier heroes whose achievements had thrilled me in the pages of the Boy's Own Paper.

Uppermost in my mind, however, was the necessity for achieving academic success, for it was essential that I justify the faith placed in me both by the headmaster and by my parents. Then there was the question of that Paston Scholarship. That had to be won at all costs. It was this thought which superseded all others when, on my first day, I took my seat in Form 2A and heard the voice of our form master droning out the names on the register. "Abbs, Allen, Bacon, Bagshaw, Bird . . ." It was a formula which was to be repeated many hundreds of times in the coming years, with almost unvarying monotony. Even as we progressed through third, fourth and fifth forms the composition of our little group changed very little, and it soon reached the stage where we would have been quite capable of intoning our responses in correct sequence without the reading of the register.

We soon became accustomed to being addressed merely by our surnames for, having reached such an advanced stage in our development, Christian names had become mere superfluous appendages. Even out of class, the boys mostly used just surnames, although a few were treated to the honourable familiarity of a nickname. It was, in fact, only a matter of days before I had inherited the traditional family title of "Baggy", just as my father and brothers had done before me.

One of the most significant features of those early weeks, however, was the gradual realisation that I had arrived at Paston with a reputation for excellence in both academic and sporting fields. At first I found this rather pleasing, for it brought me a degree of respect from the other boys and, indeed, from some of the masters. Such a reputation, however, would have been difficult to live up to even if it had been self-earned. The trouble was that it stemmed not from any personal ability which I possessed but solely from the achievements of the three brothers who had preceded me. They had all shone in various ways, and it soon became apparent that I was expected to emulate all three in every facet of school life.

Arthur, though not perhaps taking the school by storm, had done well in both form room and sporting arena and had then gone on to study dentistry. Even at that moment he was on the verge of being the first Pastonian to qualify as a dental surgeon. Stanley never shone as a sportsman for, with his mind on higher things, he would forget that the ball was there to be either hit or kicked. Academically, however, he must surely have been one of the most naturally brilliant pupils ever to pass through Paston. Peter, two forms ahead of me at that time, earned his School colours at both football and cricket and had no difficulty in satisfying the masters in matters of learning. Furthermore, his almost universal popularity resulted in his winning the Trafalgar Shield, awarded annually to the most outstanding boy in the school.

That, then, was the basis of the completely unwarranted reputation which had preceded my arrival at Paston. It was anticipated that my career would be a consummation of all that had gone before. In short, they expected perfection in everything. As my brain steadily absorbed this fact, I developed a strong desire to be first. Even worse, I became scared of failure. For a while I managed to cope with the situation, though later it was to bring me much heartache.

I suppose the feature of my new life which made the strongest initial impact on me was the very length of our school week. In the first place, I faced a 15-mile rail journey each way to North Walsham and it was thus necessary for me to leave home at the unearthly hour of 7.30. On a normal day I would arrive back at around 5 p.m., though there were occasions when it would be 6.30, or even 8.30 if I had been prevented from catching my normal train. Then there was the fact that we did a six-day week.

Wednesdays and Saturdays were loosely designated as "half-days", but these were, in fact, devoted to sport. The fact that sport was compulsory meant that nobody could escape. Most of us had no wish to escape, but there were many who had neither the inclination nor the ability to engage in any form of sporting activity. For them, those afternoons were periods of agonising misery from which there would be no release until the end of their schooldays. Those of us who derived pleasure from sport, however, threw ourselves into those twice-weekly matches with great enthusiasm. For us, even in our junior years, there was always the burning ambition to represent our house and, further ahead, the greatest pinnacle of all, a place in the School First XI. I cherished strong hopes in that direction, and I applied myself willingly to the task of developing the skills of football and cricket.

There was, however, one event in our sporting calendar which filled me with loathing, an emotion which was, in fact, shared by the great majority of my schoolmates. This was the annual cross country race which was run over a circular course which began and ended at the School House. I have forgotten how many miles we had to cover; I remember merely that it was too many for my liking.

The strange fact is that, although I have always been endowed

School House at Paston. The "migraine seat" (see Chapter 19) occupied a sunny position facing the tennis court.

with a marked degree of patience over most things in life, that quality never came to the fore in my attitude to sport. My philosophy always was that, once I was involved, I wanted to get quickly into the action and get on with it. I suppose it was this attitude which largely accounted for my comparative lack of distinction as a cricketer for, as a batsman, I was never content to dig myself in at the start of an innings. My one ambition was to hit the first ball as hard as possible and to continue treating each one in the same manner. Occasionally this policy was successful and, by frightening the bowler out of his wits, I was able to notch up a reasonable score. More often than not, however, disaster would strike rather early in my innings and my stays at the wicket were mostly notable only for their brevity. My approach to football was rather similar for then, as a centre forward, my great aim was to get on the attack and do my utmost to get the ball in the opponents' net.

When it came to athletics the effect was even more dramatic, and I became renowned as a sprinter. I was almost unbeatable over 100 yards and the 220-yard race usually saw me breasting the tape in first place. Even the 440-yards came just within my compass, but anything longer than that I treated with utter disdain. As for the School Mile, well, the thought of pounding four times round the track in a steady war of attrition against one's opponents struck me as being an utter waste of time.

That being so, I think it is understandable that I regarded the Cross Country race with a marked feeling of dislike. That feeling was, in fact, common throughout the school, for there were only a handful of boys who actually professed to enjoy it. We regarded it not so much as a sporting activity but, rather, as just one of the traditional dates in the school calendar, like Speech Day and Founder's Day, which had to be tolerated. Nobody ever did any training for the event and, as participation was compulsory for anyone with the minimum qualifying requirement of having two legs, I sometimes think we must have presented a sorry sight as we straggled our way through the countryside.

To me, the one redeeming factor concerning the race was the fact that the middle section took us across Felmingham Heath, that wild tract of land which had captivated me in my earlier childhood. I thus devised a system of running which would at least enable me to enjoy part of the afternoon's activity. As we set off from the school along Aylsham Road, I would go straight away into a sprint. I knew I would be unable to keep it up for very long, but it enabled me to reach the heath well before most of my colleagues. Then, finding it necessary to take a breather, I was able to relax on the heath and, indeed, to check on the progress of the orchids and sundews, together with anything else which caught my eye. By the time I had done this I had, naturally, been passed by quite a large number of runners. At that point it was necessary for me to summon up my remaining energy and make for the Norwich Road and the finishing leg back to school.

I suppose it is not surprising that the best position I ever achieved was when I finished in 25th place. To the unenlightened observer, that may not appear to be a particularly brilliant achievement. At the time, however, the fact that I, as a sprinter, had finished in such a high position in a field of 103 runners gave me an inner feeling of satisfaction. It must be admitted, however, that the only real pleasure we derived from the race was when we arrived back at School House and knew that we would not have to undergo the torture again for another twelve months.

With the exception of that particular race, I engaged in all possible sporting activities with great enthusiasm. I suppose there were two reasons for this, first and foremost being the fact that I enjoyed every minute of it. The other factor which influenced me was the realisation that the winning of academic laurels was not necessarily an automatic passport to achieving the admiration of one's schoolboy contemporaries. They were much more likely to be impressed by sporting prowess.

It was in the academic field that I most wished to shine, however, and, as one term succeeded another, I worked steadily towards that goal. I had no great difficulty in such subjects as mathematics and literature, for I had acquired a fair knowledge of such matters as St. Mark's. I found great interest in my first introduction to real science subjects, and I was, likewise, not unduly bothered by my initiation into the mysteries of French and Latin. None of us were particularly keen on Latin, but there were to be many occasions in later life when I was thankful that I had acquired an early knowledge of the language.

Thus it was that my early months at Paston sped past in an atmosphere of unruffled calm. My enjoyment of life was further enhanced by the fact that, after two terms, I had come top of the form on each occasion. At last I began to believe that there really could be a chance that the governors might give me that coveted Scholarship.

It was at this point that I decided to enter for one of the prizes given annually for original work outside the normal curriculum. I was by no means sure that I could find sufficient time to complete such a project, for we were regularly burdened with large amounts of prep. There were two subjects every night, each supposedly needing 45 minutes study, and three at weekends. This already meant that there was never time for Boy Scouts or similar youth organisations.

Nevertheless, I set myself to the task and I chose the Eccles Prize. This prize, bearing the name of a former headmaster of Gresham's School, was for natural history, and I decided to present a survey of Norfolk Wild Flowers. Out came my wooden presses and up went my bed to accommodate them. I sought out specimens by the dozen and there were times when I almost needed a step-ladder to climb into my bed. Each pressed species was then lovingly stuck in a notebook and surrounded by written details of form and family, habitat and lifestyle. When the time came for the submission of entries, I had filled seven books. It is a matter of regret that those books were never returned to me, but my disappointment over that small matter was soon forgotten when I learned that I had won the Eccles Prize, just as Arthur had done before me.

Then, as my first year approached its end, I learned that I had also been awarded the Form Prize. My cup of happiness was just about full to the brim.

I then decided, however, that I would try for one further achievement by entering for the Elocution Prize. This involved reading a selected piece of literature before the entire school, and I settled for the opening chapter of "Martin Rattler", one of my favourite books at that time. The judging was in the hands of a group of our masters and their announcement at the end of the proceedings was to bring me disappointment. I had, apparently, come a close second. Later, my form master was to take me aside and, surprisingly, tell me that the panel of judges had, in fact, considered that my performance had been the best. In view of the fact that I had already won two prizes, however, they thought it fairer that another boy should get this one. "I feel sure you will understand", he said. Frankly, I didn't understand. I felt distinctly cheated. From that day on, I never again entered for any of the special prizes.

Speech Day that year was, for me, a very happy occasion. Twice I was to mount the platform and receive a prize and a handshake from the Chairman of the Governors. Then, as we neared the end of the proceedings, the Headmaster stepped forward and declared that he had a special announcement to make. It was the one piece of news I most wanted to hear. The Governors had awarded me the Paston Scholarship. My entire body was overcome with a glowing feeling of warmth such as I had never before experienced.

We sang the School Song with gusto. We sang the closing hymn with even greater enthusiasm. It was the same hymn which we always sang on the last day of term, and it was the only one which ever received the full power of our combined lungs. The very rafters vibrated in unison as we poured forth those much-loved words: "Lord dismiss us with Thy blessing".

Thus ended my first year at Paston. Gradually, we all dispersed and, as I set off on my journey home, my heart was filled with happiness and a strong feeling of the goodness of life.

CHAPTER 17

The Staff Common Room

The most striking thing about the staff at Paston was the tremendous feeling of continuity which they exhibited, for there was very little chopping and changing. Major Pickford and Captain Brown; "Rod" and "Wamps"; "Emma" and "Cherry" – nobody could remember the time when they hadn't been on the staff and everybody knew that they would go on long after we had all passed by. It is true that an occasional new master arrived, but then one of two things would happen. Either he would disappear in a flash as quickly as he had arrived or he would take root and become firmly entrenched in the establishment, unlikely to leave until he was carried out.

Major Pickford, an army officer in the Great War, was our headmaster and, as such, was usually accorded the correct degree of deference. Very rarely did we refer to him by a nickname although some of the more rebellious characters might call him "Sticks" (an allusion to his somewhat spindly legs, seen at their best when in his army uniform) or even "Narrer" (derived from the overall slightness of his build). Most of us were quite content to call him "Percy", but even that term of endearment was shunned in the hearing of other members of staff. Major Pickford always appeared to conduct the duties of his high office in a somewhat distant manner but, probably because of his military background, he nevertheless enforced a strict code of discipline.

His form of discipline was by no means based on fear, but rather on respect. He was certainly not a flogging head. I can only remember him administering the cane on one occasion and this was when one of the boarders stole a stamp collection from one of his dormitory colleagues. The offender was publicly given six of the best, after which he was made to say "Thank you, sir" to the Head and was then summarily expelled. I suppose there are many modern advocates of human rights who would condemn this action as barbaric. I would not now wish to pass judgement. I know that, at the time, most of us were filled with a feeling of revulsion, but I nevertheless believe that there are many hundreds of former

Pastonians who, in later life, have had cause to feel thankful for the discipline which was forced upon them in their boyhood.

The two Hare brothers, "Wamps" (because of his large feet) and "Rod" (because he never spared it) could strike terror into young minds by their very presence, whilst Captain Brown, responsible for physical training and woodwork, had the spasmodic habit of presenting a stern facade which fooled nobody.

"Wamps" was our purveyor of history, which he put over in his own forthright manner. It was also his annual duty on Empire Day to regale us with a lecture on "The Development and Significance of the British Empire". We all derived much pleasure from this talk, largely because we knew that, on its conclusion, he would convey the Headmaster's wish that we should have the rest of the day off.

He is most remembered, however, for his bunch of keys. This was the weapon he used to express his displeasure at unsatisfactory work. While his pupils were busy over their exercise books, heads bowed and pens striving to put sensible sentences onto paper, he would wander through his flock. Every so often he would pause behind an unfortunate scribe and, over his shoulder, read what was being written. If what he saw pleased him, he passed on to another, but the slightest sign of displeasure brought the bunch of keys down on the back of the miscreant's skull. I could never decide which was worse – the stinging blow from the keys or the few eternal seconds which preceded it as one waited for the weapon to reach its target.

"Rod's" name was earned by a different weapon. Metaphorically he ruled his charges with a rod of iron, but in reality it was made of a different material. It was, in fact, a long wooden pole which he kept near his chair and with which he could attack even the furthermost of his pupils. Any unfortunate boy who dared to incur the master's wrath would find himself on the receiving end of a swinging blow from "the rod". The effect of this was worse at the back of the room; we all tried to sit near the front, for it was not an easy weapon to control at close quarters. At worst, one was likely to suffer merely a glancing blow whilst, on a lucky day, it might be just a near miss.

The other weapon in "Rod's" armoury was verbal attack accompanied by a dry, sardonic wit. The sound of a test tube or flask crashing down and splintering on the floor of the chemistry lab would bring forth the cry of "Yes, my friend. Those things are made of glass. They neither bounce nor bend!" Failure to satisfy him with the standard of one's work would cause him to declare: "Your knowledge of chemistry wouldn't allow you to pass a public house, let alone a public exam". These gems of wit, delivered in his own unique style, evoked gleeful chuckles on the first few occasions that we heard them, but they were repeated with such frequency as to become somewhat irksome and we found ourselves automatically miming them with him.

"Pardoe" Brown, another former soldier, took us through an ill-assorted variety of pursuits. He was the perpetrator of our mid-morning physical training torture, he led us in more conventional exercise routines in the gym and he did his best to instil a modicum of military discipline into the Cadet Corps. The most tangible result of his efforts, however, must surely have come as the result of his woodwork classes. There can be few homes in that part of north-east Norfolk which do not contain a selection of badly made knife boxes, clothes horses and rolling pins.

"Cherry" Harris (he of the rubicond nose) emitted an aura of bonhomie as he led us through the intricacies of algebra; "Streak" Lachlan, tall and thin, appeared at all times vaguely non-committal, even when it was patently obvious that none of us would become Latin scholars. Miss Lumb, the only female member of staff apart from Matron, took us for Art, and her feminine intrusion into our otherwise secure male bastion was grudgingly tolerated. We called her "Emma", plus one other nickname which I will not commit to print.

Our second language was French, the mysteries of which were painstakingly revealed to us by "Vic" Manwaring. "Vic" was patience personified and I think most of us developed a reasonable skill in understanding the language, though most of this was confined to the written form. When it came to carrying on a conversation, we never progressed beyond the stage of thinking in English and then trying to translate as we went along. This slowed things down somewhat and the resultant conversation was hesitant in the extreme.

At one point, the Headmaster decided that our progress would be helped if we had the services of a real native French teacher and, accordingly, he announced that such a person would be coming over at the start of the following term. This caused quite a stir, especially when a rumour spread through the school that the new teacher was to be, in fact, a female. The phrase "French mistress" conjured up all sorts of images in our minds and we began to think that, from now on, learning French would be fun. Our high expectations, however, were shattered when "Monsieur" arrived and proved to be a very ordinary little Frenchman. Furthermore, the mutual difficulties which we and he were to encounter resulted in his stay being a very brief one.

In the first place, the words he used, though identical to those we had heard from Mr. Manwaring, had a totally different sound which completely mystified us. Then, to compound the agony, it soon became apparent that the sound of his native language being daily manhandled by his pupils was more than the poor man could stand. Our fractured French , delivered with more than a hint of a Norfolk accent, drove his patience to breaking point. He stayed with us for just one term.

It fell to Norman Cutting, that illustrious figure in the musical world of North Norfolk, to initiate me into the delights of his beloved art, but he and I knew that he was on a loser right from the start. The Bagshaws have always been notoriously unmusical and, after all, had he not previously attempted the impossible with my three brothers? It was not that we did not appreciate music (nothing could be further from the truth) but we just couldn't produce it in any form. None of us played any kind of instrument, and, when it came to vocal effort, if one of us had ever hit two correct notes within the space of ten bars it would have been an event of earth-shattering magnitude.

Mr. Cutting accepted defeat with the finest of good grace. He tolerated my unproductive presence at our form's music periods and, when it came to singing, he told me not to bother to join in but to mime to the music produced by the others. I became so expert at this that I sometimes think that, if I had been born a generation later, I could have made my fortune as a pop singer. During my boyhood and early youth I mimed to some of the largest backing groups ever assembled together.

There were two other members of the teaching staff who made their impact on me in greatly differing ways. One was Mr. Drakes, who came to the school from Lincolnshire and was to double up as Geography and Sports Master. Before his arrival we were regaled with tales of his sporting prowess. Soccer, rugger and cricket – he was proficient at all, and it was reported that he had played for his county in the Minor Counties Championship. We awaited his arrival with impatience. I am not sure whether his sporting skills were as great as legend had claimed, but certainly he was to play a great part in the development of what latent talent we possessed. He was the sort of master for whom one never attempted to invent some sort of jocular nickname. His initials were T.E.D., so he soon became, and always remained, just "Teddy".

I only remember two cloudy intervals connected with his presence in the school. The first was shortly after his arrival, when he inaugurated a campaign to abolish soccer and introduce rugby as our winter sport. We all resented this. We had always played with a round ball and we were violently opposed to the change. Eventually, however, our fears were allayed with the announcement that soccer would continue. It was rumoured that a change to rugby would have meant the purchase of new goalposts, an expense which the school could not face. Whatever the reason, we were happy. We didn't want to play rugby – not even for Teddy!

The only other occasion on which he and I were in disagreement was during the course of a football match when our opponents were Bracondale School, from Norwich. The match was played to the accompaniment of heavy rain and a biting wind, which made conditions unpleasant in the extreme. Suddenly, I had the ball at my feet and I went charging through the opposing defence with the intention of notching up a brilliant solo goal. Unfortunately for me, their goalkeeper had other ideas and he advanced to meet me. Realising this, I decided to stop my forward dash and use more subtle means of attack. Sadly, however, the muddy conditions made stopping impossible and, as I skidded helplessly forward, my progress was only halted when my body hit that of the goalkeeper with a sickening thud. Then, as I collapsed in the mud, I felt a searing pain go through my chest.

I lay on the ground in agony as the ball was cleared to the other end of the field. Then, from the touchline, I heard Teddy's voice ordering me to get up and get on with the game. This was impossible, so I summoned up all my remaining strength and pulled myself off the pitch. Teddy was there immediately, towering over me. If I expected sympathy, I was to be disappointed. He dragged me bodily to my feet and pushed me back on the field of play.

I cannot think how I managed to get through the remainder of the match, nor how I survived the train journey home, when every jolt sent a wave of pain through my body. However, sympathy then arrived in the shape of my father, who declared that what was needed was a good rub with embrocation. Then, grabbing a bottle from the kitchen shelf, he began to apply it with great vigour. The pain from this operation was infinitely greater than anything I had yet suffered, but I tolerated it, for I had great faith in my father's knowledge of these things.

It was later diagnosed that I had suffered a broken rib. I took great pleasure in acquainting Teddy with this fact, but he remained unimpressed. His view seemed to be that, even if it had been a broken leg, I should have carried on until the other one gave way!

The other new arrival was J.B.L. (I will go no further than his initials). J.B.L. was a Londoner whose firmest conviction was that the best way to instil discipline into his pupils was to browbeat them into submission. He administered impositions rather in the manner of a Lady Bountiful distributing largesse to the poor. And a hundred lines was never sufficient for him. Always it was at least two hundred and sometimes as much as five hundred. We had no objection to two hundred for, by tying two pens together in the proper manner, they could be done as quickly and easily as a hundred. But five hundred was unacceptable – it just didn't fit the system.

J.B.L. had an accent which was somewhat foreign to us – we didn't come across too many Londoners in those days. He had one phrase which he continually used throughout each period of maths instruction. At frequent intervals he would pause in his discourse and enquire, "Is that roight?" Sometimes this would be repeated as many as thirty times in one session. This became such a fascination to us that, prior to his lesson, we all placed bets on how many times he would say it. One of the boys acted as bookie and recorded our wagers, all made in the form of cigarette cards, which were still our major form of currency. I often think that J.B.L. must have been impressed by the copious notes we made during his lessons. Whenever he looked at us we were busily putting pen to paper. Little did he know that we were recording each repetition of his magic phrase, "Is that roight?"

The main reason why I personally disliked J.B.L. was that, as soon as he arrived and for reasons known only to himself, he took a great personal dislike to me. I never found out the reason and I can only say that the feeling was mutual. The situation was such that, throughout his stay (which was mercifully brief) we engaged in a sort of constant cold war which occasionally hotted up. Each of us was dedicated to trying to get the better of the other. Needless to say, he was in the position to be the most frequent winner. It was not until the end that I eventually achieved my greatest success.

When he was about to leave the school, no announcement was made and the matter was kept completely secret. Presumably he was to leave after Saturday morning school and on Monday we would carry on as though he had never been there. Our central information service was very efficient, however, and every boy knew about his impending departure at least a week before it took place. Thus it came about that, on the Friday afternoon, he accused me of some misdemeanour. I pleaded my innocence, but he would have none of it and ordered me to write "Five hundred lines – by tomorrow!" At last my chance had come. I knew he was leaving on the morrow and I felt sure that the last thing he would be thinking about then would be collecting an imposition from me. Perhaps I was taking a chance, but it came off. I never wrote the lines and he never asked for them. Even now I can remember the feeling of smug satisfaction which I experienced that day. I had won the last battle!

Those, then, were our mentors in those youthful days at Paston. I have a sneaking suspicion that the pictures I have painted of the occupants of the staff common room may carry more than a hint of disrespect. If so, I can only plead that, at that age, the attitude of most schoolboys towards their masters is tinged with a certain degree of disrespect, at least on the surface. Inwardly, however, those worthy people all gained our affection in varying degrees, and there are many generations of Old Pastonians who have cause to acknowledge with gratitude the manner in which they were prepared for their entry into manhood.

It was in 1606 that Sir William Paston had set up his educational establishment to provide Norfolk boys with "godly learning to guide their wills; arithmetic, writing and grammar". My four years within Paston's walls were but a fleeting moment in its long history. To me, however, they represent a significant era during which the things I learned did not all come from text books.

CHAPTER 18

Playing At Soldiers

One of the strangest institutions at Paston, and one which most of us strongly disliked, was the Cadet Corps. We never could quite see the point of it all. However, our officers were three of our masters who had served in the Great War, so presumably they considered it beneficial for us to be treated to a modicum of military discipline. We, however, could never see it that way. It was not that we were conscientious objectors or anything like that. It was just that the whole concept seemed so childish and futile.

To begin with, there was the uniform. To the unenlightened onlooker this must have appeared comical in the extreme; to those of us who had to wear it, it was also excessively uncomfortable. Beginning at the top, there was the cap. This was obviously army surplus from the Great War, for it was of the familiar peaked variety as worn by members of the expeditionary force when they first crossed to France in 1914. The regimental insignia on the front had been removed and replaced by a metal representation of the school badge, but that was the only difference. Furthermore, as these caps were handed down to successive generations of boys, we were lucky if we received one which was anything like a good fit. I never liked wearing headgear of any kind, and mine was so tight that, after a parade, it inevitably left me with a red, inflammatory ring around the middle of my forehead which took several days to subside.

The upper part of one's body was encased in the tunic, which was hooked tightly at the neck, buttoned all the way down and then given extra support by a stiff wide belt. The tunic was also a legacy from earlier military campaigns, possibly even as far back as the Boer War. It certainly made no concessions to comfort, though it did ensure that the wearer kept his body stiff and erect. One could not possibly do otherwise, for it was as restricting as any whalebone corset.

If my description so far suggests that our uniform was somewhat strange, I must warn the reader that the worst is still to come, for the lower part of one's body was encased in khaki shorts. These were made of the stiffest material imagineable, rather like a kind of starched sacking. Furthermore, it was not just the stiffness which made them uncomfortable, but also the fact that the material was of an extremely bristly nature. If one had been lucky enough to be issued with a pair which were too large, the effect, though comical, was not too physically punishing. In my case, however, I received a pair which, besides having a tendency to restrict the flow of blood to my nether regions, set up such a high degree of bristly friction that I count myself fortunate to have escaped without permanent physical disability.

Beneath the knees, the ensemble was completed by black shoes and a pair of puttees. Each puttee, a length of khaki cloth of interminable length, had to be wound around the leg from ankle to knee, always finishing in the correct place so that the pair matched. This, in itself, was a kind of Chinese torture which took an age to complete.

It will be seen that donning this outfit was, in itself, an affront to human dignity. Is it little wonder, then, that, having done so, we showed little enthusiasm for parading in that attire in a public place?

There were many aspects of the cadet corps which puzzled us, but the one which we found most difficult to understand was that, although we daily attended school in long trousers, we were required, when playing the part of fighting men, to do so with bare knees. It was not only the embarrassment but also the risk of physical injury. We were quite safe when parading in the Yard or on the School Field, but when we went on manoeuvres in Bacton Wood or on Felmingham Heath, there were always the hazards of trailing brambles and hanging briars which hooked into the skin and readily drew blood. Above all, however, it was the indignity of the get-up for, though the good folk of North Walsham had seen it all before and never gave us a second glance, there were occasions when we journeyed further afield among people to whom our appearance was quite a novelty.

There was the occasion in 1935 when I was selected to play football in the English Schoolboys team against Belgium in Brussels. Naturally, members of the team came from all over the country and it was decided that the schools to which we belonged could each send a group of some 30 to 40 boys as supporters. As we were to be housed in the Grenadiers Barracks in Brussels, it was decreed that we must all travel in our cadet uniforms. Thus it was that, at the appointed time, some four hundred young soldiers gathered at Dover ready to make the crossing. Needless to say, we were the only ones wearing short trousers.

We suffered the catcalls and jocular comments of our new-found companions with the best possible grace until relief came in the shape of a widespread epidemic of seasickness which gave them something else to think about. By the time we reached foreign soil we were all feeling better and eagerly anticipating coming events. Eventually, the ferry docked and we disembarked with full military precision and lined up on the quayside. There were many Press photographers recording the scene and we were somewhat flattered that the majority of them made straight for our little group from Paston and were snapping us from all angles. We were thrilled to think that photographs of us would be in the Belgian newspapers.

The next day, as soon as we could escape, we dashed out to buy all the papers we could find. We opened them one by one and, sure enough, each of them had a photograph of us impressively displayed. The only trouble was that not one of them included our faces. Each one carried a close-up of a long row of bare knees. Oh, the shame of it all!

I always tried to hide the secret of our cadet uniform from friends and neighbours in our home village. This was by no means easy for, on the days of our frequent parades, we were required to travel to school in uniform and spend the entire day thus attired. I therefore adopted the practice, irrespective of weather conditions, of wearing a raincoat and carrying my peaked cap in my school bag. Even in the heat of summer I could be seen walking down the main road and round the corner to the railway station with that coat concealing my guilty secret. Not until similarly-clad figures boarded the train at Wroxham and Worstead would I remove it.

I suppose there were about a hundred or more of us in the corps, and the majority of us were classed simply as foot soldiers. There was, however, a select little group of about eight boys who constituted "The Band". When I use the word "band", I do so in the loosest possible sense, for the sounds which emerged from their instruments were not so much a form of music as a kind of primitive tribal rhythm which was supposed to assist the rest of us in our marching. And, believe me, we needed all the assistance we could get.

When we marched in the yard things were not too bad, for the sound of our boots on the asphalt spurred us on and the fact that

The bare-kneed soldiers of the Paston Cadet Corps.
Rail travellers on the nearby line had a grandstand view of our military activities.

the Yard was of a pretty regular oblong shape helped us to keep in a straight line. On the playing field, however, it was a different matter altogether. The grass muffled any sound which might come from our marching feet and, even worse, the fact that the shape of the field bore no resemblance whatsoever to any kind of geometrical form made straight lines mere figments of our imagination.

This problem was destined to have a profound effect on my military career when, after about a year, I was inexplicably singled out for promotion and I became a lance corporal. Wearing that single stripe on my sleeve gave me a certain degree of pride, but this pleasant feeling soon left me when I realised that my high rank meant that I had become what was known as "right marker". This meant that I was required to march on the extreme right hand side of the front rank of four cadets, with the others all following behind. Furthermore, everybody took their position from the right marker and I was thus responsible for the orderly progress of the entire corps as we marched across the field.

Perhaps the responsibility was too much for me, or it could have been that my heart was not in it, but somehow I just couldn't manage it. I would think I was doing rather well when, suddenly, Captain Brown's voice would bellow across the field: "Right Marker – keep a straight line". Sometimes he would introduce a little variation with "Where are you heading for now, Right Marker?" or "Right Marker – send me a postcard when you get there!" He always addressed me as "Right Marker" rather than by my name, but that was no consolation, for everybody else knew who the right marker was. Eventually it became too much and I began to crack under the strain.

Another bone of contention was the fact that we were required to carry out our full parade irrespective of weather conditions. Even in extremes of blinding rain and swirling snow we plodded our way across the field while Captain Brown barked his orders from the shelter of the pavilion. The members of the band were not so harshly treated for, although they normally practised outside, the first spot of rain would see them also scurrying into the comparative comfort of the pavilion. This was not out of consideration for their physical well-being but rather to prevent damage to their instruments. This struck me as being a blatant example of unfair discrimination and I therefore decided that, taking all things into consideration, there was only one course of action open to me. I must get myself transferred to the band.

Now, it was well-known that my musical talent was not one of my greatest attributes, being more or less on a par with my ability to march in a straight line. It was clear, however, that Captain Brown could not wait to find a new right marker for, within a remarkably short time, I became a bugler in the band.

This, incidentally, produced another slight complication, for my mother did not take kindly to the idea of my playing an instrument which had been in such close proximity to somebody else's mouth. She was sure I would catch something. However, after giving the mouthpiece an all-night soaking in Lysol, she declared it to be sterile. Unfortunately, the smell of disinfectant was so strong that it was only after hanging it up in the fresh air for several days that I was able to put it to my lips. Then I was able to join the music makers. I cannot claim to have raised the standard of performance of the band, but I have always possessed a good sense of rhythm and this was much more important than worrying about which notes came out of the instrument.

Being a member of the band had another great advantage when our cadet corps went into battle with the corps from Yarmouth

Grammar School on our annual Field Day. The idea of Field Day was that, in the morning, one school corps would defend a certain area of land against an attack from the other, and then, after a break for lunch, the roles would be reversed. We found it all rather baffling, particularly as we had no firearms and, when we caught up with the enemy, we had to clap our hands to simulate gunfire. An adjudicator would then appear and give his ruling upon which side had come out on top in that particular incident. It all tended to remind us of games which we had outgrown in early childhood.

The advantage which we, as band members, enjoyed was that, as our musical services were not required, we were allowed to take our bicycles along and act as messengers. This meant, in effect, that we could ride at random through the countryside, making sure that we kept away from the enemy lines. We then merely had to make sure that we kept the rendezvous at the chosen location for lunch. Our masters always ensured that the lunch break was taken conveniently near a local hostelry and it was because of this that I almost fell headlong into disaster on my last Field Day.

Our headmaster had left his package of sandwiches on the grass verge while he sought liquid refreshment and I inadvertently rode my bicycle over them, flattening them beyond recognition. Then, as I looked down at the uninviting remains of his meal, the Head suddenly emerged through the doorway of the pub. It was in that fleeting moment that I acquired one of the basic skills of soldiering – the ability to dissolve into the countryside, using natural cover as camouflage in order to escape detection.

I am afraid the Cadet Corps and I had little to offer each other. Perhaps that is why, in later life, I was to join a Service which wore a blue uniform rather than khaki.

CHAPTER 19

The Reality of Life

The book which I had received as Form Prize at the end of my first year was "The Three Musketeers". It was a fine volume but, although it still occupies a proud place in my library, I have never experienced a desire to read it for a second time. It was, however, a different matter altogether with the Eccles Prize, for this was Gilbert White's "Natural History of Selborne".

I had never heard of that particular book and I knew nothing of its author. As soon as I opened its pages, however, I fell under his spell and marvelled at the extent of his observation of the natural world. I tried to visualise that little eighteenth-century parson travelling round his parish and conscientiously writing down his notes and comments concerning everything he saw. Then, for a century and a half, his letters had been not only preserved but also made available to all true lovers of rural England. That book immediately became my favourite above all others, and it has remained so throughout my life. I have read it more times than any other book in my possession, and each time with increasing pleasure and admiration.

Gilbert White's book had apparently gone through nearly a hundred editions since the author first saw it through the press in 1789. The edition which I received was to give me added delight because of the fact that it had been edited by Cherry and Richard Kearton, with added photographs which naturally had never been available to Gilbert White. The Kearton brothers were noted naturalists and had long occupied a high position in my list of boyhood idols. Some time earlier I had, in fact, met Cherry Kearton when he had been to North Walsham to present a film concerning the life of the Golden Eagle. I was one of the privileged few who were allowed on to the stage to talk to the naturalist and, furthermore, to touch the live Golden Eagle which he had brought with him. I still remember the incident with pleasure, for it was the only time I have ever seen a Golden Eagle.

When I first held Gilbert White's book in my hands I was just thirteen years old and I suppose it was inevitable that my mind should immediately be captivated by the thought of devoting one's life to the study of wildlife. It was a tempting thought, but I cannot truly say that it was my childhood dream, for I knew that it was a dream which could never be realised. I forced my mind to forget it, for I knew all too well that my future had already been planned for me. It had been decreed that I was to follow my eldest brother into the dental profession. It was an age when the nature of one's future life was arranged by one's elders, and it would never have crossed my mind to query their decision. Thus, there were certain targets to be reached and pre-determined standards to be achieved. The first such target was my School Certificate, but that was three years into the future. At the time, three years seemed an eternity.

It was against this background that I entered the Third Form and began my second year at Paston. My life continued through largely untroubled waters and, though I was not destined to win the Form Prize that year, the fact that I was never out of the first three places caused great satisfaction all round. My progress at sport also continued unabated and, by the end of that year, I was playing football for Nelson House and had also reached the giddy heights of the School 2nd XI. It would, in fact, be true to say that, through-out the remainder of my school career, none of the tribulations which lay in wait for me were sufficient to upset my sporting accomplishments. They were soon destined to play havoc with my academic progress but, during those brief afternoons of football and cricket, I gained temporary relief from the worries which were steadily bearing down upon me.

It was not long before I gained a place in the School First XI at both football and cricket and I eventually won my School Colours at both sports in two successive seasons. I suppose my greatest success was when, at the age of 15, I was selected to play football for the English Schoolboys XI in the match against our Belgian counterparts to which I referred in the previous chapter. This was, in fact, a double thrill for me for, at that time, I had never once ventured outside the borders of my native county, let alone put my feet on foreign soil. We lost the match, but that in no way detracted from our enjoyment of the occasion. Overseas travel was much more of a rarity in those days and our trip was a privilege enjoyed by very few. With typical boy-like unkindness, we all agreed that the sight of our sports master being violently seasick on the return journey put the final seal of success on the occasion.

At this time I had also taken up tennis and had developed a modest degree of proficiency at the game. I therefore decided to enter for the School Tennis Tournament and I surprised myself by reaching the semi-final. I was then drawn to play Henry Cox, a player of outstanding ability who had, in fact, played in the junior tournament at Wimbledon. He was easily the best player in the school and I knew that I had not the slightest chance of beating him. Nevertheless, I looked forward to the match, unaware of the fact that my exit was to come about in a rather unfortunate manner.

Our game was scheduled to take place on the School Field at 4.30 on the day in question and I accordingly made my way there ready to do battle. An hour later, however, my opponent had not arrived and, as I had already missed my normal train, I decided to catch the next one and then, the next day, to claim the match by default. It was as I was leaving the field that I spotted the figure of Cox approaching me, accompanied by, of all people, the Headmaster. I should, perhaps, explain that, while I was a day boy, Cox was a boarder, and there were big differences. Anyway, the Headmaster demanded that I return and play the match. I explained that to do so meant that I would not be home until almost 9 o'clock and I then had 1½ hours of prep to attend to.

It then transpired that the reason for my opponent's late arrival was that, in company with the other boarders, he had been doing his prep in the library. I would gladly have done the same thing if it had been possible, but the library was out of bounds to day boys. I put it to the Headmaster that, as I had been on court at the appointed time, surely I was justified in claiming the match by default. His response was predictable but, nevertheless, slightly unnerving. He almost exploded with indignation and retorted that he had never heard of such a thing.

To this day I marvel at my temerity for, at that point, I gathered together all my reserves of courage and said, "In that case, Sir, I wish to scratch from the tournament". With that, I turned and left the field to catch the train which was just pulling into the station. I had no regrets at being out of the tournament, for I knew that, if we had played, Cox would have wiped me off the face of the court. It was the manner of my dismissal which gave me a feeling of remorse, together with the fact that I had incurred the Headmaster's displeasure.

In all honesty, I believe the Headmaster had anticipated what my reaction would be to my opponent's non-arrival on court and that was why he took the unprecedented step of acting as Cox's chaperone. To my fellow day boys, however, it was another example of what we considered to be the preferential treatment afforded to the boarders. We realised that they lacked the comfort and comparative freedom of home life, but we nevertheless felt that they had certain priveleges which were not available to us.

Firstly, of course, they did not face a long journey to and from school and then, at the mid-day break, there was always a hot meal waiting for them. We had no school meals and had to make do with sandwiches. Furthermore, we were not allowed to eat them on the school premises. Thus, while the boarders dined in the comfort of the refectory, we made our way up to the School Field where, in the shelter of the pavilion balcony, we would munch the contents of our greaseproof-paper packages. At one time a fish and chip restaurant opened in the town and, once a week, we would take ourselves there and enjoy the luxury of a sit-down meal. Unfortunately, news of this soon reached the Headmaster and the restaurant was declared out of bounds.

We envied the comfort in which the boarders partook of their meals, just as we envied the fact that they were allowed to do their prep in the peace and quiet of the library. Some of us would have gladly availed ourselves of this facility for, though it would have meant catching a later train, at least we would have arrived home happy in the knowledge that we had the rest of the evening free.

Then, of course, there was the figure of Matron hovering in the inner recesses of School House and tending to the needs of her young charges. It was generally felt that, for a day boy to come under her motherly care, it would be necessary for him to at least break an arm or a leg. It was towards the end of my third year that I approached an unhappy period when I would have benefitted from a little care and understanding from somebody such as Matron.

To this day I am unable to think of any reason for the change which took place in my hitherto untroubled passage through life. I only know that my final year proved to be one of almost unrelieved tension and unhappiness. It began with the gradual realisation that I was not achieving the standard which was expected of me. No longer was I in the top three places. Soon I had dropped almost halfway down the form. It was not because I was not trying. In fact, it was rather the reverse, but the more I strived to overcome my difficulties, the worse they became. I would spend long evenings studying page after page of history or geography and I would retire to my bed happy in the knowledge that my brain had absorbed all the necessary facts. Then, in the morning, would come the sudden realisation that, overnight, all that knowledge had slipped away. There would then be a frantic effort on the train to try and retrieve the situation, but never with the degree of success I would have liked.

It was at this time that I first became a victim of the misery of migraine. The attacks would come at least once a week and were to cause even further disruption to my studies. I feel sure that the masters had no knowledge of the unpleasant nature of the condition. There was hardly one who showed any great degree of understanding and there were one or two who, in fact, gave me the impression that they regarded me as a malingerer or, at best, a bit of a nuisance. If I had been a boarder, I could have reported to Matron and found a haven in the dormitory or, at least, within the shady recesses of the library. As it was, however, the onset of an attack would lead to my being sent from the formroom and told to go and sit on "The Seat". This was a wooden bench by the side of the drive at the front of School House.

It could be said that "The Seat" was in a very pleasant situation, for it received the full power of the sun as it pursued its orbit through the sky. It was an ideal spot for watching a game of tennis on the nearby court, but it was not the best of settings in which to sweat out the rigours of migraine. As my eyes became filled with flashing lights and throbbing pains bounced through my head, I would lay prostrate and wallow in a deep sense of self-pity. This feeling was, in fact, made worse by the knowledge that, in my absence, my form mates were having a test on some subject or other. They would be accumulating marks which, because of my absence, would be denied to me. There were many occasions when I would wish that, by some miracle, I could go to sleep and not wake up any more.

The disruptive nature of my schooling at this period of my career was naturally destined to have a serious effect on my progress. As the date of the School Certificate Exam came inexorably nearer I put every ounce of effort into an attempt to regain lost ground. In the end, however, the result was to be the one which, in all honesty, I knew to be inevitable. Although I did well in certain subjects, I did not achieve a sufficiently high overall standard to enable me to pass on to pre-medical studies. The fact that a large number of my colleagues fared even worse did nothing to ease my disappointment, for many of them had no need of such a qualification for entry into their chosen careers. For me, however, it was a vital necessity.

My last day at Paston was one of very mixed emotions. As I made my final exit, however, my uppermost feeling was one of anti-climax. Somehow, I had lost all sense of purpose. I no longer knew in which direction I was heading.

It might be thought that, after that final year, my affection for Paston would be, to say the least, muted. Once I had untangled my brain, however, nothing could have been further from the truth. I looked back at the old School with affection and gratitude, for it had taught me much. Within its walls I had acquired a knowledge of a wide range of subjects. Above all, however, Paston had taught me something which was never listed in the curriculum, namely the Reality of Life.

Henceforth I was determined to be master of my own destiny. If there were to be targets to reach, they would be targets which I myself would set. If ambitions were to be realised, they would be ambitions which I would choose rather than those imposed upon me by other people. It was in this frame of mind that I set about the task of planning my future.

My first decision was that I would forget all about the School Certificate and would, instead, tackle the College of Preceptors Examination. This demanded a slightly higher standard, but it was an examination which I could take as an independent candidate. Furthermore, if I could achieve credits in seven subjects, the door would be open to pre-medical studies. I enrolled for a correspondence course, acquired the necessary text books and made a full study of the syllabus. Then, by planning each week's work, I found that I could allow myself the occasional luxury of a game of football or a visit to the cinema. Some six months later I savoured the heady glow of success with the acquisition of those seven credits.

The next step was the Pre-Medical Examination in Chemistry, Physics and Biology. This involved another correspondence course, supplemented by daily attendance at Norwich Technical College. There, in St. George's, I joined a group of young students whose objectives were similar to mine. We worked together as a jolly band of seekers-after-knowledge until, in due course, I was once again able to satisfy the Examination Board.

At last I was on my way and then, after a successful interview with the Dean of the Medical College, I entered the portals of the London Hospital to start my professional training. Three further years of study lay ahead of me before I could achieve my final goal. Furthermore, those years were destined to be full of incident for, quite apart from the normal demands of student life, the country was on the verge of another war.

The little Norfolk boy had come a long way since he had cried in the Picturedrome and searched the country lanes for Old Shuck. Much had happened since he had wandered the countryside with his friend Billy and dodged that flying flat iron in the Salvation Army Hall. Much more was still to happen as he took those last determined steps towards manhood.

But that, to borrow a well-worn phrase, is another story . . . . .

Acknowledgements

Most of the illustrations are from photographs in my own collection, but I am indebted to the following people who have given assistance with additional items: Judy Ball, for George Swain's photographs on pages 120 and 123; Beth Corston (page 48); Mike Ling (pages 28 and 45); Stratton Long, for Harry Tansley's photographs of the *Sepoy* rescue (page 23), and Clifford Temple (page 125).